New Lives for Old

by

Fenton and Evelyn Babcock

RoseDog❖Books

PITTSBURGH, PENNSYLVANIA 15222

RoseDog Books
701 Smithfield Street
Pittsburgh, PA 15222
Visit our website at www.rosedogbookstore.com

ISBN: 978-1-4349-8604-7
eISBN: 978-1-4349-7599-7

New Lives for Old

by

Fenton and Evelyn Babcock

Authors' Note

Due to our personal limitations, we completed all the text with assistance in transcription. We are greatly indebted, therefore, to the following ladies: Sue MacKenzie and Joan Smallwood for this critical stage of the writing production.

Assistance in overcoming our physical limitations came from many members of the Westminster-Canterbury staff. The nurses and physical therapists could not have been more helpful to our project.

Fenton's sister and daughter reviewed, tested, and improved it, as did Evelyn's son.

Highly valued technical assistance in preparation of photographic support came from David Greene and Robert McAllister. For the loan of one of his tandem bicycles, we are indebted to Spencer Riding.

As in our writing before, encouragement came directly to this project from the librarian at Westminster-Canterbury, Warner Eliot.

Foreword

This book is made up of two independent memoirs that come together in the final chapter. Woven throughout these memoirs are literal and imagined encounters between the two authors that point toward the last chapters, which bring together these two authors into one, new identity.

We chose a bicycle built for two as a metaphor for our relationship because of the need for mutual direction, strength, and cooperation in order to successfully ride such a bicycle. We thus invite you to ride with us on our tandem bicycle onto the beautiful Golden Gate Bridge for the first encounter of the book. As we ride along in the morning fog, which fortunately lifts momentarily, looking down, we see two things. First, the attack transport ship USS Menifee, which was on its maiden voyage down from Oregon where it was built, in Astoria. As the ship went under the Golden Gate Bridge on the famously large swells that come in from the Pacific, one of the sailors on deck happened to look on the starboard side to the shore and saw there, at the famous and historic Presidio, standing in its beautiful old chapel, a lovely young lady waiting to be wed. Thus for the first time, Fenton and Evelyn, having come across 3,000 miles of the continent, might have seen one another for the first time. Having gone ashore, Fenton walked with fellow sailors to the Chinatown streets that are always so attractive for tourists, and amongst the tourists, there probably was Evelyn.

So now, Dear Reader, you are underway through these two memoirs. Keep your eyes ready to spot one or more encounters between us as we moved more or less in parallel for more than fifty years. Ultimately, we came to live in the same life care community in Winchester, Virginia.

Table of Contents

Preface

Tarry awhile with us, if you will, and go in time with us in tandem down the memory lane that time has built for us two. Some eighty years are covered in these parallel memoirs. They had been written by us individually, with little crossover opportunities for you to use if you wish to. They bring out the seemingly, almost amazingly, close encounters that we had over the years. But during your reading, you will come to realize that we joined our hearts together only in the final stages of our lives. In so doing, we looked not only back onto our many experiences that are recorded here, but also into the future that we believe we have found for ourselves after the death of our respective spouses.

In the course of this tandem writing experience, we have found ourselves guided by an ancient Chinese philosophical construct entitled "Ai Chin," translated as "enduring love."

The chapters you will find addressing respective bases in our lives. You will then move onto those chapters that show the development of our careers. Then you will find us entering the present circumstances within which we live, which have so greatly stimulated the writing of this book. Specifically, this life together in a beautiful little cottage within a life care community, we have found ourselves engaging in a great deal of self-insight. Through the type of completely open conversation that we have pursued, we have found the desire and the strength to reach out to one another and, ultimately, reach the decision to join our lives together in marriage.

By, in effect, reliving through our old lives together, we have found our new lives together, and under the approach of Ai Chin, we have found that we are now a new persona, and in that persona, we have an outlook that is very stimulating indeed and very satisfying.

The photographs and the original poems sprinkled throughout the book are designed to convey some of the flavor that has been prudent in our lives, which ranges all the way from one extreme to another. The flavor of our lives extends all the way from the cost and horror of the Second World War to the pressures and requirements of our professional lives, and finally, to the adjustments and relative quietude of our lives amongst wonderful neighbors with comparable, similar backgrounds in the nature surroundings of the Shenandoah Valley and the life care community in which we live. Throughout this record, you will find the approximate balance that is found and felt between the dependence upon one's self and the dependence upon family and friends to bring about the changes that are desired and ultimately required in one's life.

In the many frank conversations that we have had as a couple over the last several years building up to our marriage, we have explored the paths that we followed in order to arrive at our present location. In each of our cases, we had exposure in our earlier years to family needs involving nursing crisis and also the high expenses of full-time nursing in one's home. It was quite natural then that we would both have ended up in this life care community where we have all that we need right here and all of the medical and family support that has made Westminster-Canterbury so attractive.

In the course of those conversations that are reflected in the book, there has been a development of self-insight that has benefitted each of us individually and as a couple. The actual decision to write this book and the process of bringing it about in the tandem approach are direct reflections of the thought as a new persona involving us together.

A New Life for Old

In story, we merge our way with the concept and realization of an ancient Chinese philosophical statement. Upon the loss of our respective late spouses, at about the same time, we turned our thoughts to the future and focused on the concept of "Ai Chin." We moved steadily well beyond the state of friendship into the realm of the new life that we now share together. In reaching this state, we proceeded slowly and carefully to reach out toward one another and realized that we had a new responsibility to do so very carefully and with a firm base under our feet and with full communication between us as to what we were doing and where we thought we were headed. In our case, we sealed our entrance into this state of complete love, of Ai Chin, to marriage four years ago.

This book lays out the two amazingly parallel paths over more than fifty years that led both of us to this wonderful new state in life.

Writing separately about our backgrounds and experiences through our years of growing up and becoming married and proceeding through our professional development, we found points at which our life might have crossed directly but by chance did not. And then, ultimately, the very fortunate blending of these two paths together in Shenandoah Valley Westminster-Canterbury.

In the early chapters, we go back to the seventeenth century where both families' countries were moving prospectively southward in Evelyn's case, and westward in the case of Fenton.

The stories of our lives proceed through this century and years of growing up; in Evelyn's case in Moorefield, West Virginia, and in Fenton's case in Pasadena, California. The two like paths then came together in Northern Virginia and nearly merge in the City of Fairfax in the environs of Washington, D.C.

The retrospective coverage of our careers gives years in New York City, shows the crossovers in our lives, and we jump then to our lives here in Shenandoah Valley Westminster-Canterbury. It then references Fenton's several years overseas with his agency until his retirement, and the immediate area where we now live.

The process of writing independently preserves the separateness of our thoughts and actions until they intertwine naturally in the years leading right up to the writing of this book. And so the power of Ai Chin in forming the new life we share together is revealed.

Our purpose in writing is to pass on this experience for the benefit of family members and friends.

Prologue

Having tarried briefly in the Preface section for this tandem memoir, we offer herewith a balancing act on two lives, which we have come to believe were truly built for us and which are forming steadily into one. Those products are presented here in parallel and with some crossover capability.

Each memoir begins some whole continent away from the other, but the family bases involved have strength that is comparable and has enabled a look outward in each case. Over many years of professional career development and in the aftermath of spousal losses in both cases, there has been a combined look inward and a look together outward toward a new life for us together as a new persona, replacing the old lives.

This book thus begins with Evelyn's account of her family arriving in the seventeenth century in New England and turning its eyes southward, to the southeast branch of the Potomac River and the beautiful valley of Moorefield, West Virginia. Some of her family photographs herein show the beautiful architecture of that early period, when the family purchased property from one of the land grants to the British Lord Fairfax received from Queen Elizabeth.

Evelyn's account of her own birth and early family life captures the lore of that period and the beauty of that relatively small valley situated in West Virginia, which complements that of the Shenandoah Valley in the State of Virginia.

I, Evelyn, thus tell you how those beautiful old, large houses were constructed of the locally made brick and inside preserved the old, beautiful architecture of that early period.

I go on then to describe the strength and closeness of my former early American family. You, the reader, will live with me through my earliest years and my growing-up experiences, which are interrupted by the Great Depression and the family moving to Richmond.

At this point in our book, Dear Reader, you are invited to carefully mount our mythical, classical bicycle built for two, and ride it across what we will call the "Golden Gate Connector." That leads to Fenton's side of the book and his account of his family base and the first, nearly miraculous account of the two parties, Evelyn and Fenton, being together in a close encounter. Having viewed this miraculous, near encounter from the Golden Gate Bridge looking down on the San Francisco Bay below, you are now ready to read through Fenton's account of his family base and his growing-up years in Southern California.

In Fenton's initial part of the book, he undertakes to match the nearly unbelievable claim by Evelyn and offer this claim on my part. For she claims to have remembered as a newborn child the fact that there was a snowstorm going on at that time and I am claiming something much more unbelievable. That is the fact that I was in a baby carriage at age one, looking up and seeing the Spirit of St. Louis plane piloted by Colonel Charles A. Lindbergh as it dipped its wing over my family's home in Hoquiam, Washington.

My father, Thorpe Babcock, having been brought up in Milton, Massachusetts, and schooled at Yale University, turned his back on the family history of involvement in the Revolutionary War and other aspects of life in New England. He reached the West Coast, entered the lumber business, and became a manager of a lumber mill at which the manager had a very nice, old house wherein I was born and brought up.

The Great Depression, having driven the family to California to start a new life, is where my memories really begin, and the nearest that I can recall, is the train ride from the State of Washington to California and our life beginning in the small city of Pasadena. My father's book, entitled Broke at Forty-five, tells that whole story of his life as a beginner in the business of lumbering and his building of a whole new life for himself and his family in the State of California. For me, the difficulties of the Depression were balanced by the warmth and great promise of our family life.

My account will document the quoting of poetry by my father as he would stride through the living room and the beautiful music produced by my mother at the piano and the accompanying singing by my brother, father, sister, and me and the playing of the violin by my brother.

My account includes focus in my mind upon the Naval Academy as the goal for growing up, and the accompanying studying and physical development that obviously paid off for me in the subsequent years. My three years of combat at sea during the war caused me to change my goal to the study of international relations at Yale University. It was there, in the class of 1950, that I was soon caught up in the lore of New England and the lore of Yale itself, the challenge of intercollegiate rowing, and intercollegiate boxing before entering graduate school. I was to learn four lifetime lessons: need for clarity and purpose, requirement for loyalty in action, benefit of open conversation, need for endurance and love. At that point, our reader is encouraged to mount up on the bicycle built for two again and cross over to Evelyn's side of the book. There, you will read of Evelyn's life as a child, an adult, a married person, a mother, and the development of Evelyn as a trailblazer in the field of primary and secondary education in the area of Northern Virginia.

My involvement in this lengthy process involved taking advanced degree courses in eight different institutions and teaching at a wide variety of levels, in addition to carrying managerial responsibility at a variety of institutions. A report on the launching of kindergarten schooling in Virginia was published.

Here, a branch that Evelyn offers you as the reader back to Fenton's side of the story is an account of travel on the Greyhound buses from New York to Virginia and back on a weekly basis. For Evelyn, that came in the course of a one-year assignment representing Virginia on a special group planning kindergarten development. That group in New York was located at Columbia University, very close to the place where Fenton was then working in New York for the Central Intelligence Agency. He was also riding the Greyhound bus weekly back and forth to work from Vienna, Virginia. Evelyn, having worked for the Greyhound Company in renting pillows for people who would be getting on to a bus, my weekly round-trip between Manhattan, New York, and Fairfax County in Northern Virginia became an easy routine.

While we can record no encounter between us on the bus circuit, it does seem strange indeed that we were again in an encounter of sometime pointing towards the present life that we have together.

Hi, this is now Fenton waving to you from our bicycle built for two and I am taking you through the story of my professional career in the Central Intelligence Agency, which is from my graduate years at Yale University. My lifetime experience in the CIA is recorded in considerable detail in the book, A Mercurial Intelligence Career, published in 2009. I therefore focus here on the rather high degree of acculturation that I was fortunate to have first of all with my wife, Haya, whom I married in my beginning graduate year at Yale and through my work with the Chinese in Taiwan and Hong Kong during a total of twelve years for the Agency.

In this book, the emphasis is on appreciations acquired through cultural influences. From Haya, for example, I learned the steadfastness of Germans who had lost everything during the war. In those circumstances, the Germans' inclination was to pick themselves up and reform their opportunities for the future.

From my Chinese contacts and friends overseas who had lost everything on the China Mainland, I learned that for Chinese, the determination was certainly to survive and to better their circumstances in the future. For the Chinese, perhaps the least rebellious people in the world, they have the position of perhaps the most revolutionary.

New Lives for Old

Each of us looks back more than fifty years
Of marriages filled with years of hard work and accomplishments
Two separate fine families of offspring
As we strolled individually through the sands of time on occasion
We thus saw in the tides of time items to be preserved
And others to let go with the passing years
Here then are many collected memories
That formed the respective bases in our lives
On which we stood and reached out for our new lives
Following the deaths of our spouses
With the encouragement and help of families and friends.

Following an ancient philosophy
We sought enduring love (Ai Chin)
Through completely frank conversation
In seeking those aspects of married life
That had been somewhat perhaps missing
Those two examples which often fall
Prey under the stress of developing careers
Specifically frank communication
And the warmth of a familial relationship.

As the tides of time washed over our footsteps
We now saw them moving forward side by side
And we came to realize that our discussions together
Were bringing forth the challenging and satisfying conversation
That had been missing in our lives up to that point.

Having found our feet on the bases of our backgrounds
We then found ourselves reaching toward one another
In the realm of physical contact
However carefully done and diplomatically so
Then the warmth of actual love began to be felt.

The deaths of our respective spouses
Placed our relationship in a potentially new framework
We then came to realize the prospect of teamwork with this much increased productivity
And turning to our church for approval and strengthening of the developing bond
Thus discussed seriously the question of marriage.
Proceeding as we have from our marriage of June 16, 2007
We have observed that our footsteps from the sands of time
Now appear as one set the footsteps so widely foreseen
By the ancient Chinese philosophers.

As those of one new persona
Being a new persona having been so strongly cheered on
By our fellow neighbors at our life care community
We returned to the rather difficult task of producing the first book
On the Intelligence career of Fenton
And have turned confidently to the task of producing this book
On our new lives for old.

With specific contribution by members of our families
Who have detail and interest that will complement those
Made available by us for the text
The result we believe is a fairly unique one
That can have potential benefit for some readers
And certainly for ourselves has cemented our relationship
For the enduring love.

We believe we are on track for a significant number of
Additional years of a very happy life here
In our beautiful little cottage at
Shenandoah Valley Westminster-Canterbury

Being a life caring community we are thus likely to benefit in the future
Regardless of what change may be coming our way
And thus further entwining our intellects which were developed through
Long postgraduate studies and parallel career development.

Fenton Babcock

Evelyn's Memoirs

This story of my life is not meant to be an autobiography but merely relates some of the high points during the more than eight decades I have enjoyed! Some dates may not be accurate, but will be approximate—accuracy will depend upon whether the date is recorded someplace or whether it is a mental recall.

1924 - My birth
1942 - Secondary school graduation
1943 - Marriage to James Fallon
1944 - Brother Merle killed in Guam
1945 - War ended
1946 - Jimmie came to Moorefield
1946 - Son Merle's birth
1947 - Jimmie and I entered Potomac State College
1949 - Jimmie and I moved to West Virginia University
1952 - Jimmie accepted teaching job in Burns, Oregon
1952 - We moved to Oregon
1955 - Jimmie and I separated, and he moved to Japan
1955 - I accepted job in Fairfax County Public Schools
1956 - Art Valotto and I married
1956 - I received degree from West Virginia University
1957 - I entered George Washington University
1963 - I graduated from George Washington University
1966 - I entered early childhood program at Columbia University

1967 - I graduated from Columbia University
1968 - I worked in establishing kindergarten in Fairfax County Schools
1972 - I became principal of elementary school
1978 - I retired
2002 - I moved to Shenandoah Valley Westminster-Canterbury

Chapter One

Growing Up with Family Roots

It was during a terrible snowstorm in the winter of 1924 that Dr. Brooks rode his horse into the center of town, went into a small building behind a large building, and tethered the horse. He went upstairs to an apartment over the brick building and there, a baby was being born. I was that baby and the building was my father's store.

The store was located in the middle of a small village. This village had grown up in a valley called the South Branch Valley, which meant that it was on the South Branch of the Potomac River. When our family had arrived in America, they went down looking for this particular area because it was part of the land grant given to Lord Fairfax by the English monarch. Lord Fairfax, in turn, had sold part of the land to various settlers, mostly German, Scottish, Irish, or British people.

My family, the Wilsons, had land in the land grant and it was based on the River itself. They built a rather large log cabin composed of two floors for the family to live in while they decided where to build the house. They selected the site and since the land had clay which was suitable to make bricks, they fired the bricks which went into the building of the house. The house itself was of a Georgian construction with large rooms and eleven-foot ceilings on the first floor and a twin staircase that ran from the front entrance hall up to the second floor and down to the back hall. Then there was a small addition, which was attached to the rear of the house. It had a kitchen, a butler's pantry, and the family's pantry.

There were three sitting rooms: a formal parlor, a sitting room where neighbors and friends were entertained, and a smaller sitting room for the family when they read the paper in the evening or stopped to converse before ascending the stairway up to bed. A young man walking through the South Branch Valley area was an artist who was hired to decorate the formal parlor. He painted the room blue and white in such as way that there was a strong allusion of white woodwork that was not present. That was an artistic approach called trompe l'oeil, which created an allusion of reality that the viewer could not be sure was real or not.

The house was built in 1854, or in that era. My father was born in the 1880s in the house that had originally been used by the family, the log house. He grew up there and some of the family moved to another house over on the River, which was more suitable for them at that time.

The area along the River that had been claimed by various people had gradually been built up with large brick houses, and over the years, some of the families got slaves to help in working their land. One of the houses had a bright basement of brick, and with places where the owner had shackles that he used when slaves were not doing as he wished. They were taken to the basement and shackled there until he was ready to let them loose.

Our family did not have slaves or use them in any way. Instead, the young children in the family were tutored by an in-house teacher who lived with the family. The boys in the family then went out and worked the fields. One Wilson was Clerk of the Court for Hampshire/Hardy County. As Clerk of the Court, he knew when farms were going up to be sold and he bought those that he wanted. Thus when he died, he had many farms for his children. My father inherited a farm on the South Branch of the Potomac River and he had a tenant farmer living there. He would go up from town to supervise what was being done. I remember this in my early childhood.

My immediate family consisted of my father, my mother, two brothers, and myself. I was the youngest child. My older brother, Wayne, was ten years older than I. My second brother was named Merle and was just a year older than I. We were very close, almost like twins. My father was a small man; he had brothers who were much taller than he—he was about 5' 8". He was very authoritative and strict with his children. He was stricter with Merle than with me; he never struck me. I remember one incident when Merle was punished and I wasn't. It happened at our camp, which was built up on our farm on the river. While our parents were busy, Merle suggested that we go down to see the cattle. So we walked a good distance down to the house where the tenant farmer lived and were looking around when our father came hunting for us. When he found us, he directed us to walk back to the camp. He had a switch in his hand and he switched Merle almost every step of the way back to camp and he didn't touch me at all. That was the way I was always treated. I was very seldom punished. It was because of the way in which my father felt. He had wanted a daughter so badly and, after two boys, a daughter was born and she was treated as someone special.

My mother was a small woman, probably around 5' 1" or 5' 2" and was very quiet, withdrawn, possibly not feeling well often. This changed after my father's death and she became a different type of person. She had beautiful, wavy brown hair that had probably been blond when she was small. She played the piano beautifully.

My older brother, Wayne, had red wavy hair. I don't have many memories of him when I was a young child because he was so much older. He was in high school and our paths didn't cross that often. I assume we ate meals together. My memory of Wayne was when he was in college. He went to a college called Bridgewater in Virginia and was being helped financially by a cousin, Ed Friddle, in Harrisonburg. Cousin Ed owned an amusement park, a bakery, and a restaurant. Wayne worked at the amusement park in the summer and went to college in the winter. Bridgewater is a town near Harrisonburg and that is why that college was selected.

Wayne also had a group of young men who were close friends. Several of them were musically inclined, as was Wayne. He could hear a tune whistled or hummed and could sit down at the piano and pick it out. He also had a beautiful voice, which was similar to that of Bing Crosby, a big star in that day. He played a guitar, and when he married, he married a woman named Marjorie Fisher, who had a lovely alto voice and played the banjo. Together, they were involved in a lot of musical activity. When mother played the piano, Wayne, Marge, Merle, and I often made a quartet and sang. Merle's voice was that of a low tenor, and because he was young, it probably had not developed into what it would have been later. He enjoyed singing but he showed no other musical inclination at that time. He was in the church choir, as was I.

Brother Merle was not a big boy. He had a small build and golden hair. He had lots of friends at school, both girls and boys. He did not go out for sports. His interests focused on science and chemistry. He had not developed fully by the time he left home. He did not study and he was not upset at being retained in school. I was the youngest in the family and I was almost as tall as Merle by the time we were in high school. I weighed 9 ½ lbs. at birth and had brown hair, which, as I grew, had a tendency to wave. Anna, the girl who was living with us during the winter in order to attend high school, helped me in various ways including how to wave my hair. I had all the usual diseases and Merle and I often had the same disease at the same time, such as chicken pox. I remember that I had a very difficult time with whooping cough, but usually, the diseases did not bother me. Merle was very active and daring. He climbed up on the garage roof and also jumped from our front porch down to the walk. In that little episode, he split his knee across when he landed by going down on his knee. My father was very upset about this.

On our farm, in my early childhood, my father built a camp on the banks of the River and we would go up and spend time there. Merle and I loved to play out in the River. It was not deep at that point and we could wade out and sit on big rocks.

Directly in back of my father's store was a lot where my mother's father had built a house. He and grandmother were living there. In the 1920s, my father decided to build on a lot adjacent to grandfather's house. My maternal grandparents were a very welcoming family to children. We were living in the new house when the economic crash of the thirties occurred. It was during that time that my father lost his store and he became essentially unemployed. We continued going up to visit the farm and staying in the cottage during the summertime.

My mother's family had come over to this country from England or from Germany. I have never bothered to track back where their original place was. The name was Friddle, which I believe is originally German and maybe was called Friedel.

My grandfather was born in 1854 in the little town of Moorefield. He remembered the Civil War and the army troops as they marched through town. The town itself changed hands from the Northern Army to the Southern Army fifty-four times. He remembered as a young boy climbing under the porches and looking out through the lattice at the troops as they marched through town. After the Civil War, when he was around fifteen or so, he went to work for the town newspaper in setting print, which was all done manually. When he was older, he went into law enforcement and became a guard at the state penitentiary in Moundsville. It was there that he and my grandmother had a house, near the prison walls, and where my mother spent her early years.

While my grandfather was on the staff at the state penitentiary in Moundsville, my grandmother was very active in doing community and church work. This is a letter she received dated December 25, 1900:

State Prison West Virginia,
To Mrs. W. F. Friddle:
"'Tis not the value of the gift, a stranger's hand has power to tender. Neither is it the articles intrinsic worth or a jem of rarest splendor. But it is a token of respect - a thank you for (the Xmas dinner). And in the future? I wish that your entire life may be a happy one, and your home? a home of love." Resp. wishing You and Your Family a Merry Christmas and a happy New Year.
Signed
F.S.S., by a man who was in prison for forgery

We moved into the new house probably in the late 1920s. My brother Merle and I were good playmates. The children in the area turned out to be boys, there were no girls. And so, I had several years of playing with three boys—Woog, Bill, and my brother Merle. I had no problem with that, I enjoyed them. Later in elementary school years, girls entered into the picture and I had no problems with them either. So, I grew up not playing with dolls. I had several that had been given to me with some little dishes and doll clothes, but I never did play with them. I enjoyed the boys' play more than I did the girls'.

I had a tendency to being prissy with my clothes when I was growing up. I wanted clean, often starched dresses, and as I entered high school, I took over the ironing of my dresses because no one could do them just the way I wanted them ironed. When corduroy became popular in the early 40s, all the girls at school wanted red corduroy. We had a seamstress in town who could look at a picture in a catalog or book and make that dress for you. So, I wanted a red corduroy dress like my friends. However, when I was given corduroy for Christmas that year, it was not red, it was blue. The seamstress had made a skirt and a bolero for me. My father said at the time: "Do not follow the crowd, do or get what is best for you. Red is not for you, you should have blue. Don't worry about it, just wear what you have." That direction from my father has stayed with me all of my life and has gotten much more active as I have gotten older because I tried to do what was best for me and paid no attention to what other people were doing.

I had piano lessons when I was six or seven, but during that time, my father lost his store. My piano lessons stopped and I was not allowed to "pound" on the piano because the house was kept quiet. The piano was sold when the house was sold. I enjoyed dancing when I was in high school and never had any lessons, but there were a couple of boys who were good dancers. Both of them were not in school but were working. Mother's brother, Uncle Clyde, had a large room over his restaurant that had a nickelodeon. We would press what we wanted to play and did not have to use any money. This was his gift to us young people. We danced a lot. There was one boy who worked in the print shop for the weekly newspaper, and he and I became pretty good at our dancing. During my junior and senior year, I went out a lot with a boy who was in college and was several years older than I. When he would come home for the weekend or for a holiday, we would see each other and really enjoyed being together.

I had a cousin who lived in the big Wilson Manor. I called her Aunt Katherine and mother and I were there often. She gave many large dinner parties with fifteen or twenty people. I remember the first time I was asked to sit at the main table. It was quite an experience and I was very careful to follow the use of the correct cutlery and so on as I ate. I watched what everyone else did and followed their lead.

In the mid-1930s, President Roosevelt formed the Civilian Conservation Corps (CCC) to provide work for young men. They worked in West Virginia in establishing a series of state parks. When I was in the eighth grade, my father was working at the construction of the swimming pool at Lost River State Park. He was supervising the swimming pool construction. The state asked us if we would come over and live in the superintendant's house that had just been completed. They were still working on the construction of other cabins and they wanted someone there who would be available all the time. So, we went to live in Lost River State Park. The park ranger, George Flouer, lived with us and I felt as if I had another brother. In order to get to the little town of Mathias, which was where Merle and I went to school, we had to catch a ride with another boy who lived up in the mountains and drove every day of the school year. Merle and I would walk about a mile down the road to meet him, and that walk was always great fun! It was quite an experience because there were many deer around the park. There was one deer that had lost an ear due to the fact that the clip they had put on her ear to mark and count her got caught on something. It pulled half of her ear off. Therefore, we always knew her when we'd see her because she was different and we named her Effie.

We had to take our lunches because there was no lunch at school. Mother would pack our lunches every day. I always went to where the other children gathered and ate my lunch. Merle never ate his lunch. He always saved it, and on the way home, when we got out of the car to walk our mile to the house, Effie would be right there. Merle would take his sandwiches and would share them with Effie.

This state park had been a spa back in the 1880s and had had a large hotel with a bathhouse because there were mineral springs there, which made the park rather special. In the large hotel, they had wooden tubs for people to sit in the mineral water, and I assume that the water had been heated in some way so that it would not be so cold. Where the spring came above ground, they enclosed it with the type of glass that was unbreakable but allowed you to see the sulphur water that was there. This was very close to a cottage that was known as the "Lee Cottage" because the Lee family had their own personal cottage there. They would come and visit the spa and stay at their cottage.

During my junior and senior year in high school, I often visited a place on the edge of Moorefield, which had a landing strip for airplanes. I was always fascinated by airplanes. A gentleman who owned a bottling company had his own airplane, which he kept there. He asked me if I would like to learn to fly and I said, "Of course!" I got into the plane with him and we flew many times. He showed me what instruments to use and how to use them. I was ready to solo when my parents found out what I was doing. That was the end of my learning to be a pilot because I was not allowed to go up to the airfield again.

In the early 1930s, the State of West Virginia had problems in meeting its payroll and they cut the school year to six or seven months. If parents wanted their children to attend the rest of that particular school year, they paid the teacher to do the teaching. I believe I went on to school and completed that grade. I didn't have any trouble with any type of schoolwork that I remember. I learned to read at an early age and I read lots of books. My brother Merle was also an avid reader and would read quite rapidly through a book. When he was in the upper elementary grades, he was reading chemistry books for college.

We attended a church that was very near to where we lived. It was the Moorefield Methodist Episcopal Church South. I was part of the choir and we were fortunate enough to have a musical family working with us. One of them played the organ and one directed the choir. I joined the school glee club when I entered high school and enjoyed singing very much. We had a band on the secondary school level and I wanted to join. However, my family could not afford an instrument so I became a majorette. I was taught by the father of the head majorette how to handle the baton, how to throw it in the air and catch it, and other necessary skills.

I had no problems in school socially or scholastically. I enjoyed school—I loved learning to read and I liked the other students. We had no buses and no lunch served at school. We walked up in the morning, went home for lunch, and walked back to school and back home after school. Some students took sandwiches to school but I always walked home for lunch. I remember one boy was the child of a teacher and he always took his lunch. One of his favorite sandwiches consisted of peanut butter and jelly. I had neither seen one of those nor had ever eaten one. It was intriguing to stand there and smell that wonderful peanut butter and watch David eat the sandwich.

There was an Amish girl who lived at the top of the mountain; in order for her to get her schooling in, she had to live with somebody in town. She lived with us and helped with the housework—washed the dishes and things of that sort. That meant that I had no assigned tasks—I didn't help with the dishes and I didn't help with the cooking. Anna shared my bedroom and she had lovely coal-black, wavy hair. She taught me how to take care of my hair, to shampoo it correctly and how to deal with the wave.

My brother Merle had flunked two grades in elementary school and, therefore, although he should have been a year ahead of me, he was a year behind me. He was a bright boy but he wasn't interested at all in what was going on in the classroom or doing the work. He was a very rapid reader and every weekend, when the library was open, he would get five or six books, take them home, read what he wanted to from each, and return them. He loved science and worked with chemistry experiments at home.

Usually at Christmastime, he was given a chemistry set. Wayne was becoming a biologist and would go out any time he had spare time and look for salamanders, snakes, bugs, butterflies, and worms. Merle became a big part of that. Some of Wayne's specimens were sent to Carnegie because they had never been found before. Everyone in town seemed to be aware of Merle's and Wayne's collection habits. Therefore, it was not unusual to find a paper sack in the front hall with some sort of specimen inside. I remember at least once when it was a snake. Wayne made a movie for the state showing how he did what they called "milk the poison" from a rattlesnake in order to send that off to be worked into serum to be used if one were bitten by a rattlesnake.

My paternal grandparents lived on a large farm with a large brick house, but as they got older, they decided they should live in town where they were closer to the doctor. They had moved into a house that my grandfather had had built in the southern part of town. Part of the river had been changed to flow down past their house and they called it the Race. They built a laundry house on the opposite side with a small walking bridge across the Race to the laundry house from the main house. They also had a large mill for grinding grain into flour and a miller's house.

My paternal grandfather died before I was born and my grandmother was both blind and deaf. I was told that this was the result of some disease that had caused her to lose both her sight and her hearing. Before that, she had been quite active and had had six or seven children. Two of the children were aunts who lived with her. They were what they used to call "old maids" and they took care of her and the house. We visited her every Sunday afternoon. It was a very formal atmosphere and we children were directed to a straight chair and were told to sit there for the whole visit. Needless to say, the warm feeling that I had for my maternal grandparents did not develop for my other grandmother. Her old age was being spent in a rocking chair in a very formal sitting room and she was told what to do by her older daughter whose name was Marie. Now Aunt Marie was very directive both with her and with anyone who came into the house. They communicated with my grandmother by way of what they called a trumpet. This was before the age of hearing aids in the ear. It was difficult even with that trumpet for my grandmother to hear anything that we children said; therefore, our communication with her was very negligible. She knew we were there and that was about it.

I became a cheerleader at school and it was fun working with other girls on how to lead the cheers during football and baseball games. The games were on land donated by my grandfather to the town for that purpose. He had specified that was the way the land was supposed to be used and no other way. By these high school years, I had become a part of a group of girls—there were six of us in the group. It was very nice being part of a group. However, I had no bicycle and most of them did, so I still wasn't able to do a lot of the activities. When I was a senior, one of my subjects was journalism and I became the editor of the school paper. I loved the writing and the teacher was very helpful in showing me what and how to do certain things.

Our house was sold during my junior year in high school and we moved to an apartment over a restaurant. I also began to work at a ten-cent store on holidays and whenever I was needed. This gave me some money to use as I wanted. At no time in my life was I given an allowance.

The graduating class of 1941 had Eleanor Roosevelt as the speaker. I was a junior and an usher at the graduation. There was great excitement for days before and after this event. We practiced several times before the graduation exercises to make sure we knew what to do and how to do it. Mrs. Roosevelt stayed overnight in one of the large old houses in the area. The house was called "The Meadows" and it was two miles out of town.

There were twenty-eight students in my graduating class. These students were mainly from the town of Moorefield, but there were a few who were brought down from the mountain. Now whether they had started buses at that time or whether their parents saw that they got down to town for their high school years, I am not sure. Some of our brightest students were from the mountain and were boys. There were four at the top of the class of 28 students who were so close together in their achievement levels that it was almost difficult to determine who would be the valedictorian and who would be the salutatorian. After that group of four boys, I was next in line.

Evelyn's grandfather, William Friddle

"WILSON FARM"
Moorefield, West Virginia

Homeplace built around 1700
Bricks were made of clay which was on the property

Evelyn's parents in D.C. in the 1920's

Back of Evelyn's mother's home

Evelyn and mother giving a champagne toast

Granville Feb 26 - 1925

Store ad in local paper by Evelyn's father.

Chapter Two

<u>Overview of My Education</u>

My educational profile is not like my husband's, Fenton's, who went to Yale University for nine years and got three degrees. I also have three degrees but not from the same university. I have attended nine colleges and/or universities:

Potomac State College
Shepherd College
Madison College for Girls (before it became a university)
West Virginia University
University of Virginia
University of Maryland
George Washington University
Columbia University
Shenandoah University

My degrees are from West Virginia University, George Washington University, and Columbia.

My first husband, Jimmie, and I went from Potomac State College to West Virginia University in Morgantown, West Virginia, where Jimmie got his bachelor's degree.

I had not been able to take as many classes because I had a small child and I wasn't able to take as many courses as he took. This meant that I had to come back to West Virginia University in order to get a degree. By that time, I had begun to realize that a degree was desirable. However, I still hadn't determined my goal of what I wanted to be in life. I remember one of my professors heard me talking to someone about the fact that I was considering going into law. He asked me to remain after class, and at that time, he talked to me about the fact that women did not become lawyers, that it was not something that I should aim for; instead, he tried to steer me into other types of things that he considered desirable for women, such as teaching and nursing.

After graduating from West Virginia University, Jimmy took a job in Oregon teaching school out in the desert. Of course, I went along and it was while I was there that I went back in the summertime to West Virginia to get my own degree. In the meantime, I was becoming very interested in child growth and development as well as how children learned to read.

The job in Oregon was interesting and they offered me a job also, knowing that I did not have a degree but needing a teacher very badly. This was for a small school out in sheep desert country. It was a two-room school and it had what they called a teacherage, where we lived. Children from the surrounding ranches came into school, the parent brought them in. Some of the boys rode their horses into town and put them in a barn near the school and then rode them home in the evening. At noontime, one of the mothers would bring in a hot lunch prepared for everyone there. We would go out to the kitchen and serve ourselves from the food brought. They had a dishwasher and we would clean up and put the dishes in the dishwasher and go back to the classroom again.

It was there that I began to be interested in how children learn to read. I followed the teacher's guide in the teaching of reading and it was amazing to see how well the children responded. This aroused my curiosity about how this happened. Some of the children did much better than others and I began to notice the fact that not all children learn at the same rate or learn the same things. The accumulation of these observations began to influence me as I took further courses when I had the opportunity. That summer, I was finishing up my degree at West Virginia University and I went to Morgantown and stayed there in order to take the necessary courses.

One of the courses that I took was Marriage and the Family. At the first class, a young Italian boy sat down next to me and a new friendship began. His name was Art and his sister and her husband were professors at West Virginia University. I went with Art to meet his mother, and several times, I had dinner with the family. I got to know them well and felt very comfortable.

At the end of that summer, Jimmy and I decided to go our separate ways. He took a job in Japan and left the country. I talked with Art's sister, Alice, who knew that Fairfax County, Virginia, was in the process of exploding in population and building many schools in order to take care of the children. Alice had been a consultant for Fairfax County, and upon her recommendation, I went to Fairfax and was hired on the spot. Art also had a job in Fairfax.

I had an apartment in Alexandria and drove from there to the area where I was assigned. Because I had taught a combination of four grades in Oregon, they were so happy to give me a first and second grade combination. I enjoyed that and spent the year getting better acquainted with Art. Jimmy and I got a divorce and so, therefore, I was free to do what I wanted to do. At the end of that year, Art and I got married and moved to Falls Church in a small house on the outskirts of town.

In looking over the colleges and universities that had courses available in the area, I found that George Washington University had a reading clinic and a degree program leading up to working in the reading clinic. In the clinic, children or adults who had problems learning to read were tested and then taught in ways that gave them assistance in learning to read.

That next year, I began going to George Washington University, taking courses in the process of reading. I drove over to the District of Columbia in order to take these courses at night and also on Saturdays. I did this while I was teaching full time, had a small son and a new husband, and therefore, a very busy life.

The Department of Instruction in Fairfax had a staff of supervisors who were divided into upper elementary and lower elementary, and also into varied courses that would work with the secondary schools, such as library, music, social studies, and science. I was observed on a fairly regular basis by both supervisors from the Department of Instruction and teachers from other schools that the supervisor would bring in to watch me teach. The staff of the Superintendant of Instruction in Fairfax was enlarging and they had an opening. They asked if I would like to become an elementary supervisor. After consideration and talking it over with Art, I decided to accept. I think my salary was between $7,000 and $7,500 the first year and that was a big sum!

There were two supervisors who worked together as a team. One worked with the primary grades and the other with the upper elementary. We had twenty-seven schools we were responsible for, working with the principals and teachers. By this time, I had completed enough to get a master's degree from George Washington University and I also began to work in their reading clinic. During all of this time, Art was very busy in his high school. He had worked his way toward becoming the head of the department, which involved all of the games and activities of physical education.

I continued taking courses, most of them in the area of early childhood. This was in the mid-60s and the nation, as a whole, was becoming interested in early childhood and the fact that many of our children would come to first grade and not be ready for even playing with other children. The government started a program called Head Start for four or five year olds. Therefore, the school system became interested in the fact that we needed to prepare our children in a better way for entrance into school, with kindergarten being the way to do that. Virginia was one of the states that was going to start kindergarten at a predetermined time.

There were several scholarships that became available for sending people into varied programs for establishing kindergarten. I was asked by our Superintendant of Instruction to apply for one of those scholarships, and I did. There were 700 applications for the particular one I applied for. There were two of us from Virginia who were selected to go. This was nationwide and once I got into that program, I found out that there were people from New Mexico, California, and all over the United States who had applied and had been chosen. I had been chosen for the one connected to Columbia University. This meant that I would be traveling to New York City on the bus and would spend the week up there and come home Friday evening or Saturday morning and go back on Sunday.

The second semester of that year, I was assigned to one of the New York City offices. Their school system was divided into sections and they had people who were staff for each section. I was attached to a supervisor who supervised schools on the Lower East Side of Manhattan. Therefore, we visited those schools, and since I had a child study paper to write, I selected a school on the Lower East Side down by the Bowery. Across from the school was a place where the poor in the area went for free meals. We visited the kindergarten classes in that school and selected one of the children, a girl, whom I would observe carefully and write a paper about.

I went down to the school at least three times a week; sometimes more than that and observed her in the classroom and then viewed other records to supplement my observation. I wrote a paper and turned it in. That was my advanced degree paper. When I had completed it and turned it in, the teacher read it and came to me and explained that a committee had read my paper and asked if they could keep it as an example of the type of paper they wanted. Naturally, I was pleased and said yes. Now I wish I had kept at least a copy of it so I would have some idea as to what I had said.

While I was down in that area, I did a lot of observing of what went on in the neighborhood. I even went over to where the meals were given and visited them during a mealtime so I could see what went on. This is a good time to say that at no time in my traveling on the subway or walking around the city did I have any difficulty. No one ever approached me or tried to take my pocketbook. Everyone was very nice, very helpful, and constructive in giving me information that I needed.

I traveled back to Falls Church by bus on Friday evening or Saturday morning and went back to New York City on Sunday, sometimes quite late. I would ride the subway up to the stop that I used for getting up to Columbia University and I walked the block by myself to the dorm. No one caused me any problems at any time.

When I arrived in Columbia to register, it was suggested that I go for a doctorate because I had the hours that qualified for that and I had my master's. I did not want to go for a doctorate for it would have meant continuing to travel back and forth to Columbia and I really didn't care about the degree itself, so I said no. So they gave me a special degree which was underneath a doctorate but indicated that I had a complete year of early childhood education.

Evelyn in elementary school

Evelyn at Graduation

Evelyn working in Richmond for Greyhound Bus Company

Chapter Three

My Career

Most of my life had been devoted to the job of teaching. I have taught from grades one through college. I had been involved in a country school, in a city school, and in teaching teachers about early childhood in an extension of the University of Virginia. Perhaps one of the most memorable places that I have taught was my first job out in the desert in Oregon. This involved children in four grades, children from ages six through eleven. There was one little boy who was in the first grade who had been kicked in the face by a horse when he was age three or four; therefore, his face was very smashed in but he was an alert little boy and settled in to read and do schoolwork.

That first teaching experience was one I will never forget, because of the involvement of the parents in the education of their children. Jimmy and I lived there in the neighborhood in the teacherage. We got to know the parents and the life of the community fairly well. It was a small community with a store, a post office, and a building that was used for community dances. We always attended those dances, and it was great fun meeting the cowboys and dancing with them and learning something of their lives.

I remember one time Jimmy, our son Merle, who was about four at that time, and I were visiting one of the ranches for the weekend. We were at breakfast on Saturday morning. The wife of the house had prepared breakfast for all of the cowboys and we were sitting at the table when someone came rushing in and said that one of the cows that was calving was having a great deal of difficulty and a couple of them had better come help her. So the gentleman of the house got to his feet and motioned to a couple of the men and they all started out to where the cow was having her calf. I immediately jumped to my feet and held out my hand for my son and took off after the cowboys. They were appalled that I would do this but I persisted and went. We got down there and watched that calf being born. It was a breech birth with the feet of the calf coming out first. The men were very skillful in helping her. This, evidently, was not a new thing for them and they knew what they were doing. So Merle and I watched this event occurring.

I also remember the dances that were held. The music was provided by a phonograph and the dances went on until about midnight and then everyone would leave about the same time.

The school was a two-room school for grades one through four and five through eight. When the children finished grade eight, they would have to go into a town and live in a dormitory until they finished grade twelve. This type of education was very new to me and I had great interest in what was occurring. I made a list of things that I really needed in order to do an effective job of teaching the children and I went to the superintendent. He looked at me and shook his head and said, "Mrs. Fallon, we don't supply all of these things and if you expect that type of equipment, then I think you had better go back east to do your teaching."

I did go back east the next year and took the job with the Fairfax County Public Schools. This was when Fairfax was in the process of growing by leaps and bounds so that we had more children in the classroom than in later years, when they were able to cut the class size down. I had a combination grade and had children who were ready to begin work in mathematics and who were ready to start reading. Other children had had no access to books, paper, or pencil and needed a lot of personal instruction. I began to recognize the stages of readiness that a first grade teacher needed to recognize in order to teach effectively. At the end of that year, the principal was transferred to a much larger school in another section of the county. She asked me to go with her and so I moved.

I have also taught adults in extension classes for the University of Virginia and was a principal of an elementary school, which was a very difficult job. The job of an elementary school principal requires many hours at the school above and beyond the regular school day. There were two incidents while I was an elementary school principal that may illustrate this. One day, an oriental woman came into our school and collapsed right in front of my doorway. She was stoned out of her head and we had no way of determining who she was and we could not get her to talk with us. Maybe we couldn't have understood her if she talked. However, she was removed by the police and I never did find out what happened to her.

Another incident was when a car drove past our school and fired shots toward the school. We were very fortunate that this did not really get into our building or didn't hit any of the people outside of the school. We never knew what happened there either. As principal, I knew the police very well and also the Protective Services. An incident involving the Protective Services occurred when a six year old came to school one day with the print of a large hand on his entire check. I immediately called Protective Services and, upon investigation, we learned that his father was a policeman. I don't know what happened with that incident either, but I was always very much involved with the police and the Protective Services.

Sometimes it was difficult to stay apart from what was happening in a child's life at home. An incident occurred when a father came in to see his small child and said that he was taking her home. We did not know that her parents were in the midst of a divorce and that the little girl was part of what they were arguing about. She had been given to the care of her mother and when the father wanted to take her home with him, she did not want to go. He said, "Yes, you are going," and he picked her up and threw her over his shoulder and carried her out of school screaming and crying. This type of work is not usually a part of a job when you are teaching. However, when you are in a leadership position, you often have to deal with problems such as this and of the child with the bruised check.

Following my year in New York City when I studied early childhood, I came back to Fairfax County and was attached to CEEC, the Center for Effecting Educational Change. It was there that I was to work in designing the kindergarten program for Fairfax County. The U.S. Office of Education awarded a $396,000 grant to Fairfax County to develop and initiate a Systematic Change Procedure going from lead studies through power programs onto incorporation in the school program. Dr. George Tankerd, Jr. was the director. I was the Kindergarten Area Study Supervisor. This was done in the school year of 1967. In 1968, we opened seven classrooms of kindergarten programs in seven different schools over the county. We had a teacher and an aide in each classroom for a half a day in the morning and then a different group for half a day in the afternoon.

The pilot kindergarten program was launched in the fall of 1967. The results of our study were published in CEEC Monograph 11, The Change Process in Action: Kindergarten by Ronald A. Dearden and Evelyn Valotto.

It was after my work with the kindergarten and getting it started that I decided that I needed to take a different type of assignment. I asked for a principal's position in an elementary school and I was given one in a low-income area. I soon saw the need to work differently with disruptive students. We did have a close association with the police and with the Protective Services. It was following my principalship that I decided to retire in 1978.

Chapter Four

World Travel

*I*n the 1950s, I was a part of the Fairfax County Department of Instruction under Assistant Superintendent Harold Ford. At that time, there were 127 elementary schools in the county and the county was divided into five areas with a team of elementary supervisors working with elementary schools in that area. There were two of us who worked with principals and teachers in twenty-seven elementary schools. Helen Haertel was my partner, and I worked with the primary teachers and Helen worked with the elementary grades. Fairfax was in the process of growing very rapidly so there were several teams like ours under the Department of Instruction.

Helen and I were good working partners, but we were also good friends and did a lot of traveling together when we could find the time. For example, we traveled to England, Ireland, Wales, the Netherlands, Italy, the Mediterranean (area including the northern coast of Africa), and southern Europe (including Yugoslavia, Greece, and Lebanon). We also traveled to many states in the United States, such as Arizona, California, New York, and Oregon.

In the mid-1960s, we decided that we should take a trip around the Mediterranean. We went to a travel agent and planned a trip. Unfortunately, the day we were supposed to leave for London, the pleasure yacht of a relative of the queen of England exploded in the North Sea. This threw that section of the world into a tizzy. Our plane was delayed in leaving New York and that made us late in arriving at Shannon Airport in Ireland. Everyplace you saw, there army men with machine guns. This made us feel protected but also it delayed us in so many places. So when we got to Shannon Airport, it was pouring down rain and we stayed soggy. We got there at 7:30 a.m. instead of mid-morning. We could not get into our room at the hotel because the rooms weren't available until noon. We had been fed continuously during the five-and-one-half-hour flight and we didn't want to eat, so we just got up and walked around several of the squares in Amsterdam.

We were finally admitted to our room. The hotel room was adequate, but you entered from the hallway into your bathroom and there we found that the shower and the commode or toilet took much effort in order to find out how they worked. So we bathed and slept for a couple of hours. When we got up, we walked miles trying to find a restaurant that Helen had been told about. We didn't locate that one but found a different one which was not frequented by tourists and the waiter was wonderful in helping us select our wine and food. We had some sort of cherry aperitif and an exotic dish of sole fixed with ginger, mushrooms, bananas, and tomatoes. All of that came to about $5 in American money.

We went on a tour of the canals all over the City of Amsterdam. The motion of the boat made me sleepy and we both decided to go back to the hotel and sleep. We were scheduled to go to a diamond cutter the next day. Amsterdam was a beautiful city and the people were nice, very helpful, and appeared to speak several languages. As we walked around, we noticed the very small roads between buildings, which were used for both cars and people and we understood why the European cars need to be very small. There were many people on bikes and many people walking.

We left Amsterdam in a cold rain and arrived in Milan in a downpour. We were not met by an agent and we needed to transfer to the train, but we did not have the tickets for the train. There, the terminals and the stations are miles apart, and since we already had the air tickets, we decided to fly. The poor man who was helping us with our luggage finally persuaded us to go downstairs in order to get where we wanted to go. The steps were carpeted and steep. About halfway down, my heel caught and I hurtled down the rest of the steps. There was a man about five steps below me and I grabbed him by the back as I hurtled down those steps. He managed to withstand my attack and to hold both of us up, thus breaking my fall. This was in view of about a thousand astonished people. I broke both heels of my shoes but nothing else. However, I had wobbly knees for several hours.

There was much confusion in the station as people attempted to help us. We did catch the plane to Venice where we waited in a small Italian café for about five hours before the customs shed opened because we needed to go through customs before boarding our ship.

When we got on board the ship, we found out they did not have our names on any list. This had not been done. Finally, they were able to assign us to a cabin which was very nice, fairly roomy with a shower, and we had a comfortable night. The next morning, we found that we were assigned a table in the dining room and that our table-mates included three Greek women, only one of whom spoke English. And of course, we didn't speak their language, but they tried to include us in the conversations. There were many courses to each meal and so much silver. They always began each meal with tea and ended with some kind of tea. The coffee was terrible. I had a difficult time eating cold cuts and cheese for breakfast. The crew on this ship was certainly international. We had American, English, Canadian, Greek, German, and Italian. And because my name at that time was Italian, Evelyn Valotto, everyone thought I was Italian and started talking to me in Italian!

We took a tour by bus that morning up very high rock mountains with narrow winding roads. Since it had poured rain the whole day, it was difficult for us. We visited a cave but I stayed outside and talked with the guide. I did not want to go in the cave. The guide who spoke in four languages had waited outside; he and I sat down and had a drink and talked.

Our trip to the mountain was about twelve hours and when we arrived back aboard the ship, we had dinner at 8:30. After dinner, we had native dancers—beautiful young people. The dancing was much in the Russian style—very vigorous. Helen and I ordered the famous plum brandy, Slivovitz, mentioned in the AAA guide, and the waiter and a girl at the table both giggled. The girl explained that women didn't usually drink it. It looked like water and burned all the way down. An American gentleman joined our table and he helped to balance the conversation.

The next morning was sunny but crisp weather. We were up at 7:00 and watched us leave Rijeka. Then we went up to the upper deck for a while and watched the scenery as we passed. We arrived at Split at 5:30 and took a tour to see the Diocletian Palace. We walked back to the ship. We sailed from Split at 1:00 a.m. and arrived at Dubrovnik at 7:00 a.m.

The next day, the weather was sunny and hot and we decided not to take the tour but to strike out on our own. It was an old city of the medieval time. We took a street car and rode miles and ended at the old city of Dubrovnik. The old city is surrounded by high walls and is very old worldly. We went into a few of the small shops and bought two brooches and a book but we wanted to explore the old city. There were many people there and we had only one hour, so we took the street car back to Dubrovnik. The walls around that old city are about sixteen-feet thick.

The next day, we were at sea and we slept all day. We got up for breakfast, went back to bed. We got up for lunch and went back to bed and slept until 6:15 p.m. We got up and dressed for dinner. Because the ship was rocking so much, it was not smooth sailing at all and was getting pretty rough at times.

When we arrived in Alexandria, we had some trouble getting clearance. We finally ended in an automobile with Mr. and Mrs. Levine from Philadelphia and Helen and me. We got a good look at the countryside as we drove around and through to Cairo. It was extremely hot, about 110 degrees. Mr. and Mrs. Levine were world travelers and were very helpful to us in talking about the area we were driving through. We stayed at the Nile Hotel. We had a big room and bath. The beds were clean but the food was poor. We went to the pyramids the next day and I decided that I wanted to climb into the big pyramid Cheops. Naturally, we saw the sphinx. It was so commercial and there were numerous beggars. An American cannot stand alone without being surrounded by hawkers and beggars who will not be put off. We climbed into the inner chamber in the Cheops pyramid. You enter a doorway and start climbing to the top. It was a very torturous climb in a crouched position. It is not tall enough for even a short person to stand upright and walk. With the accompanying heat, it was more than uncomfortable. I remember at one point I was down on my hands and knees in order to continue on upward.

The room at the top had several openings in the wall that had been made so that anyone in that room could look out and see what was going on outside.

When we had entered Cairo, they took us first to a place called Mena House, where a bank was set up to exchange money. Each of us had $5 changed and we were told that any remaining would be changed back to American money before we left the country at Port Said. Those who had some left at that time got about fifty percent of the value of their money. We felt that at this time in the mid-sixties, their money system must be in very poor state. It was against the law for a shopkeeper to take any money other than the money for that country. If a policeman or an army man was nearby, the shopkeeper would not take it. He asked for American money otherwise. If fact, he bargained for less for American money. One man at the bazaar refused to sell me a pin for Egyptian money.

When we came out of the pyramid we were exhausted; it was about 7:00 in the evening. Lunch had been at 4:00 p.m., and we looked as bad as anyone could possibly look. But we went on then to a mosque, which was a newer one and was only about 150 years old and it was beautiful! The interior of the mosque was all lined with alabaster and our guide explained the significant things to us. The outer court with a fountain being the place for cleansing one's feet, hands, and face before entering a place of worship. The enormous room with a Persian carpet was for sitting on the floor and listening to the reading of the Koran.

By the time we got to the bazaar most of the shops were closed because it was so late, but the best one had stayed open for us. The shopkeeper asked that we stay very close to her. She was a native and as we walked the streets to the shop, I was glad to obey. I would have loved to take a picture but was afraid to do so.

We arrived back at our hotel about 9:30 in the evening. Helen and I had a lovely big room with a bath the size of our dining room at home. It was fairly clean and we were glad to get a cool shower. Then we went to the ninth floor to the dining room for dinner. The waiters were very colorful in their long robes. We had ordered bottled water and it was .95 cents a quart, almost as much as a quart of wine. Mr. Levine raised quite a fuss about the prices and so did several of the other men. We found out that different groups had been charged different prices all by the same man.

After dinner, we sat out on the balcony of our room and had a brandy. The view of the city and the Nile was indeed beautiful. There was a slight breeze and the temperature became quite comfortable.

The next morning, we were called at 6:15 and had breakfast of tea and a hard roll. Then we went to the Cairo museum and this was the high point of the trip. Because of our lack of time, we had to concentrate on one area in the museum and that was on King Tut's belongings. At 10:00 a.m., we were on our way to Port Said. There were many soldiers in the area; in fact, in all of Egypt. As we left the city we were told no photographs. We went through an area of trenches, foxholes, and other very evident military preparations, which included barbed-wire fences!

Lunch in Suez was terrible! Flies were all over our food so we ate nothing and drank half of a bottle of beer. It was extremely hot. The scenery on this trip was mostly of the desert. We saw many boats along the canal area and there were many water buffalos. Our ship was anchored about two miles out and we had to take a launch. All of us were extremely tired.

When we got into Port Said, we had to go through customs and have our passes checked. We changed our Egyptian money for American coins. All of our money had been spent for water, so we waited in the office. Then we took a launch out to the ship, which was about one and one-half miles at sea.

We landed at Bayrouth, Lebanon (which is the local spelling), and what a delightful change. It was much cleaner and the people were so nice, although they pestered you to buy. We saw much bigger cars here and more of them. Many of us did not take the tour. We walked around the town and looked in the shops. I went to a store recommended by a friend of mine and bought some very lovely things. Several other people knew of that shop and said he was the best in the whole area. Since Athens and Rome were so high for tourists, I decided to buy most of my purchases in Bayrouth. We came back at noon and then went out again. We must have walked ten miles. We finally came back to base and changed for dinner.

We visited Cyprus, Crete, Athens, and, for a short time, Dubrovnik. Then we went on to Venice. Cyprus was interesting but not a place to be visited again. Crete was a lovely island, a place to spend six months if you can afford it. Scenery is beyond description, lovely beaches and some famous ruins. We spent more than half the time there in a museum.

In Cyprus we did not take the tour, but ten of us Americans hired a taxi and rode to various spots. We visited an old Norman castle built by the crusaders in the third century. It was an amazing place.

Athens was a great disappointment. We had visited the acropolis on our last visit there and we wanted to spend a day roaming the city, which was so commercial and so geared toward scalping the American tourist. Even the American Express company was geared that way. I went in their office to cash some of my American Express checks and they were charging me .85 cents to cash $100! I gave them a lecture about charging me when I had bought those checks from them. The charge for cashing was not in the plan when I bought the checks and I refused to cash them!

Perhaps the highlight of the trip was the night of the masquerade ball aboard the ship. Dinner was to be at 7:30 p.m., and at 7:00 p.m., when I was dressing, a knock came on the door and the hostess came in without waiting for an invitation. "You are to sit at the captain's table tonight. What are you wearing?" Her manner insulted me but I retained my composure and indicated the dress that I had laid out, thinking that I was wearing that dress regardless of whether she approved or not. It was a white, silk jersey with a pleated overskirt of blue. She approved and left, saying that Helen was to sit there, too, and asked if I would tell Helen that. When I found Helen on the deck and she explained to me that she was sick and on her way to bed, she asked to please excuse her to the captain.

After I dressed, I went to the dining room door and before the captain entered, I explained Helen's absence to the head waiter. He threw up his hands in horror and rushed down the steps. The captain appeared almost immediately but no one else. And since he could speak little English and I no Serbian, we stood there in silence. We were eventually joined by a French couple who also spoke no English. Two Lebanese gentlemen and a Yugoslavian ambassador to Egypt appeared. When we went to the table, I was placed between the ambassador and one of the Lebanese gentlemen. Both were charming men. The latter of the gentleman would not identify his occupation except to hint at some government connection. However, I observed later that everyone jumped at his mere suggestion, so I accept he was someone important. When his name was given to me, I did not understand it.

After dinner I thanked the captain, said that I had enjoyed talking with and meeting the other guests, and left. Since Helen and I had been invited to sit at a reserved table with Mr. and Mrs. Levine, I was going up there. But Norma, a girl from New York, said she needed help with her costume and asked if I would come and help her. So I went to her cabin. Soon that door burst open and the hostess came in wringing her hands and saying, "You must come. You are keeping the ambassador waiting!"

I explained that I had a previous engagement with Mr. and Mrs. Levine and that I could not sit with the ambassador. She said that she was sorry but that I must sit with the ambassador and that she would explain this to the Levine's. Later, when I came out of Norma's room, I went toward the club. The ambassador was out in the hall smoking a cigarette. I nodded and went in to the club. All of the gentlemen at the captain's table stood and all of the gentlemen at Mr. Levine's table stood! I was expected at both places! So I decided not to create an international incident, but to trust an American to understand my predicament. I went to the captain and excused myself for a moment and went to Mr. Levine and explained in a brief sentence or two. The hostess had not been to see them! Then I went back to the captain's table for the evening!

The ambassador was clearly in charge but not in an obvious way. He spoke English very well. He had never been stationed in Washington and had been stationed in Russia. We discussed philosophy, Freud, culture, and women. He did not dance. He explained he danced with no woman except his wife and asked if I would please dance with the other gentleman at the table. I did so, and enjoyed talking with all of them. At 1:30 a.m., the ambassador indicated that he was going to retire, said goodnight, and left. The captain had ordered sandwiches about ten minutes before this—this order was forgotten as he retired! I was free to go also!

An amusing incident happened in choosing the winner of the masquerade. I asked how they would be chosen, if it was going to be done by three judges. The ambassador translated this to the captain and then told me laughingly that it seemed we were going to be democratic and vote. We had a laughing verbal exchange concerning this. Later, when the winners had been announced and most of the people at our table were dancing, the ambassador continued his discussion by saying, "Do you see the results of voting? It is obvious that the one who won the first prize was not the most beautiful, don't you agree?" I said, "Yes, I did, but in a democracy and with voting, the best person did not always win." He said, "Ah, yes, but you have had one great man elected, President Kennedy." It was an evening I would always remember.

I had coffee with the Levine's the next morning and they were interested in every detail. The captain had eaten only two evenings in the dining room and it was some sort of honor to be chosen to eat at his table. None of us understood why Helen and I were chosen!

That afternoon, we had a bingo game following the tea hour. I missed it but Helen said that it was a great trial to sit through that bingo because the numbers were called in five languages!

When we arrived in Venice, I was impressed by the city. We were met by two different travel agencies. Our travel agent had been busy! The hotel was beautiful and we had a spacious room overlooking the canal. The service was excellent. We walked to St. Mark's Square and stopped in the small shops, had a beer at Florians, and visited St. Mark's Church. Mosaics in the church were almost unbelievable. The ceiling and many of the walls were covered with beautiful mosaics. A lot of gold was used in making of them. We had dinner on an open terrace overlooking the canal. That was the first acceptable food in two weeks, I felt. We went to bed immediately after dinner.

We ended our tour in Rome and I began to feel very tired. I looked forward to getting home. Probably the most tremendous experience of that trip was going through the Corinth Canal or the canal going into Piraesus. I managed to climb up to the top deck, which was not for passenger use, and I got a first-class view of what was happening. The sides of the cliff were several hundred feet high and the passageway was only eighty feet wide. Naturally, I did not have my camera and I would not climb down all of the ladders I had to climb up in order to get there because I might lose my place and I didn't want to miss anything either.

Another trip that I took that I enjoyed very much was to England, Ireland, and ended up in Wales. In England, we went through many of the cathedrals and I enjoyed that. In one, we heard a chorus practicing and that was beautiful both visually and auditorily.

In Ireland, probably the place that I remember most was visiting the Castle Blarney, which has a large stone and it is said that if you kiss that stone you are able to use smooth talk in a flattering and coaxing way. The section of the castle containing the stone is at the top of a tall, spire-like tower with iron bars extending into an opening in the wall where the large stone is suspended over open space. The visitor hangs upside down while her feet are held by a guide. Almost everyone who goes through that castle wants to do that because it has been known for years that the Blarney Stone is very helpful with your smooth talk.

I went on to Wales when I left Ireland and it was in Wales that my friend lived. Leonard and Dorsey Baynhan had bought a cottage in Wales and they spent a large part of their summer there each year. Dorsey had been my editor when I was with the Fairfax County Schools. She was with a part called CEEC, which meant the Center for Effecting Educational Change, that Fairfax County had set up. They had gotten some government grant money for that and it was there that I was developing the kindergarten program for Fairfax. Dorsey was the editor for all of the things that I wrote, which would be published by Fairfax County. She and I had gotten to be good friends and she was an excellent editor. I never felt any hesitation about her looking at what I had written and correcting it where necessary.

Helen had left me in London because she was going to go back to America rather than to Wales. So, I was very much alone. I rode the bus from London to Wales and that was several hours of getting to look at the surrounding countryside to see Wales.

When we arrived at their cottage in Wales, I realized that it was a thatched cottage, which meant that instead of our usual type of roofing, it had a roof made of grass, which had been bound together and then a roof made out of it and put on the building. Many of the small cottages had that type of roofing.

Their cottage was small but very comfortable. I could understand why Helen had not been invited to come and visit them also. The cottage was much too small for two additional guests. We visited several places during the next few days and one thing that I was interested in looking at a great deal was some cloth that they made of wool and was woven into varied patterns. You could use that cloth on both sides because the pattern would be reversed on the underside. They used varied colors in making these. I bought some of the cloth, which was yellow and brown and white, and then another one was brown and orange and red; the material was simply beautiful. I used it in making table mats of varied sizes for the dining room or breakfast table.

After four or five days with Dorsey and Leonard, I knew that I needed to get back home. I went back to London and caught my plane to New York. I left with the feeling that the British Isles is a remarkable, interesting place to go.

Our ship going through the Corinth Canal

Evelyn being held upside down to kiss the Blarney Stone

Chapter Five

Planned Retirement

Art and I had bought a house on the outskirts of Manassas, and for the first time, I had time in which to do a little browsing downtown. I also established a relationship with the church and started going regularly to the Episcopal Church in Manassas. I began doing needlepoint and I particularly enjoyed swimming in a swimming pool in our yard. I had never had any swimming lessons during my life and no one had ever shown me anything about swimming. I just taught myself how to move my arms and legs and I did very well in swimming back and forth in that 20 × 40 foot pool. There was a seven-foot fence around the pool area, which meant I was screened off from the eyes of the neighbors.

I worked quite a lot with needlepoint and decided to take classes. These classes showed me different types of stitches that could be done with needlepoint, and I worked on that using the canvas that had the picture already imprinted on it. I followed that for a while and decided that I really could do better myself, and so I began designing my own picture as well as using the stitches that I had learned in many different ways. I also knitted several sweaters and enjoyed just living.

We had three dogs and two cats in Manassas, and one of the dogs was a Great Pyrenees. She had a long white coat and got almost as big as a Saint Bernard. She was not quite that tall as her legs weren't that long. She had the nicest disposition with us, although there was jealousy between her and our small female wire-haired terrier. One time, when I had both of them in the car, Sunny, the Great Pyrenees, grew very unhappy with the small wired-haired terrier, and they started snapping at each other. I got in between them and ended up with seven bites, which caused me to go to the emergency room in the hospital!

One sunny June day, I was out working in the yard when a UPS delivery came to deliver a package. I didn't answer the doorbell; however, when she heard our radio working and a motor running in the backyard, she came around that way, opened the gate, and walked into the yard. Sunny came out of the pool area and bit her in the arm when she swung around to go back out the gate. I offered to take her to the doctor or the emergency room. One puncture wound was visible. She called her office and was told to finish her route, and then go to their doctor with a bill sent to us. We gave her Sunny's vaccination date and the incident ended there. However, I'm sure she probably never went unannounced into a fenced-in yard again!

It was also during this time period in Manassas that I began to entertain quite a bit. On May 30 of that year, I planned a buffet for some invited guests and Art's staff. He was still working and wanted to have his staff come out to swim and enjoy the pool area on a spring day. I was told to plan for fifty people. Here was my menu: for drinks we had available gin and tonic and beer, and to eat we had sliced ham, roast beef, baked beans, potato salad, green salad, and French bread and butter. For dessert, we had Bavarian tortes which were made after one of Julia Child's recipes, a lemon date torte and an almond torte.

I began keeping a day book, which gave me a place to write down anything I wanted to keep or be sure that I remembered. It also made me aware of how often I was going from Manassas to Moorefield to work with the elderly. At that time, most of my relatives in Moorefield were getting into their late 80s and 90s, and that included my mother. She easily broke bones and I discovered that she had osteoporosis. Out of the six grandchildren of my maternal grandparents, I was the only one living. I was the only girl and there were five boys all, who had died for one reason or another.

These relatives were in two different towns and when they needed to go to the hospital, they went to different hospitals. They also lived in their own houses and had lived in that particular house for many years. These were people of the generation where the family always took care of the sick or needy. Therefore, it was expected that I would take care of my mother and it ended that I had four people that I took care of: my mother, her brother, Arno, and his wife, Gladys, and an elderly cousin who lived in Romney, which was about 35 miles from Moorefield.

Soon I was making trips from Manassas to Moorefield to Romney to Harrisonburg. I was going to Harrisonburg because this was the hospital they were used to going to. An example of a month in that year and the trips that I made are as follows:

April 30 - 200 miles
May 1 - 200 miles
May 2 - 200 miles
May 3 - 200 miles
May 4 - 150 miles
May 5 - 150 miles
May 6 - 150 miles
May 9 - 250 miles
May 20 - 350 miles
May 21 - 150 miles

I began to see that nursing homes were looming in the future for these people. There was no way I could take care of them; however, there was the possibility of two nursing homes. One in a place close to Romney, where Cousin Glenna was, and one in Petersburg, which was 12 miles from Moorefield and would involve Uncle Arno, Gladys, and Mother.

Talking with them about going to a nursing home was not easy. It also meant, once a decision was made to put them in a nursing home, that their houses and estates would need to be taken care of. Since my mother lived in a house that was hers for her lifetime, only this meant that whatever she had saved would be used to pay the nursing home, and then I would be responsible for the rest. Her brother, Arno, lived in a large house, a Victorian house packed full of furniture, and not only did he have the house, he had a small house in back that was used to store things. Uncle Arno could sell his house, but getting it ready to be sold would be difficult and would be my responsibility. Cousin Glenna lived in a house in Romney, which was not a very large house, but she had a lot of things that she wanted various members of the family to have, which meant I would be responsible for getting that accomplished, and then selling all of their houses and the contents. I discussed this with Art and we made the decision that the house in Manassas should be sold. I loved that house and I loved the life there, but I really had no choice.

My experience at auctions helped me prepare for the three public auctions I held—two in Moorefield and one in Romney. I went methodically through the house, packed up things that the person wanted, including clothing and a few other things, and then prepared the rest of the things ready to be transported outside, which was where the auctions would be held. At the auction for Uncle Arno's things, I had two auctioneers in different yards selling!

In the meantime, our house in Manassas had been sold and we needed to get out and move to Moorefield. I had loved the life in Manassas; I loved the house and particularly liked the swimming pool. One thing I remember about the swimming pool is that our son loved to swim there and he often dived from the diving board. Many times, one of the wire-haired terriers would follow him up to the diving board. When Merle dived off, the little dog would be right behind. I wish I could have caught that on film!

Chapter Six

McMechen House Bed and Breakfast
Active Retirement

When we knew we had to leave Manassas, Art was concerned that he would not have enough to do. He was a very energetic man and he wanted to be busy all the time. He had retired prior to our decision to leave Manassas and he had gotten very involved there with selling real estate and with the Lions Club. We knew we were moving to Moorefield and there was an opportunity to buy a large house in the center of town. We were planning on it becoming a bed and breakfast.

Sam McMechen built his house in the early 1800s. It was brick and had three floors plus a basement, which was also brick. Moorefield was a Confederate town surrounded by other towns that were Union. During the Civil War, the McMechen House became a way station for Confederate soldiers who were escaping from the Union forces. There was a hand-operated elevator in the back, which went directly up to the third floor. The house was in the center of town and was used by both sides as headquarters for their particular army.

When we bought McMechen House, it was an empty house with thirty some rooms. The one thing I had to do was to plan how I was going to furnish it and to get that furniture. I went to antique shops and country auctions in the Moorefield area and I gradually got the house furnished. An example of prices paid for furniture is a sideboard from an auction for one person's estate was $820. It was an early 1800s large sideboard, well cared for and beautiful. A trundle bed was $130, a single bed was $70, a chair $75. There were six dining room chairs that had needlepoint on the seat covers and they were mid-1800s and went for $55 each. Other chairs were $115 and $275. A walnut extension table that was six-feet long was $500. A lamp was $45 and a mirror was $50 and another for $85, a chair for $300. So, it would depend upon the condition of the article and where it was sold; whether it was a one-person auction sale or whether it was an auction house. In this way, the house was gradually furnished and we were in business as a bed and breakfast for ten years.

Because the house was so large, the owner, Mrs. McCoy, had made an apartment house out of it. There were seven apartments, which totaled around thirty rooms and three porches in the back plus a porch on the front. Upon entering the house from the front, you stepped into a long hall with a circular stairway in the middle, and on the right, a large room, which eventually became a dining room. On the left was another large room, which eventually became the parlor. Directly ahead was another door, which led into the anteroom off the kitchen. This small room led to the back porch and served as a place where people entering the house from the rear parking area could wait while they registered.

The kitchen itself was quite large with a big work space, which I had built in the center of the room. This had cabinets underneath and a work space on the top where I could make bread, knead it, and shape it into loaves or small rolls. There were two stoves, two re-frigerators, and a sink with a dishwasher, which would take a load of dishes through the wash cycle in seven minutes and had a place for sterilizing within. Since the kitchen had originally been part of an apartment, it also had a bathroom complete with tub and shower to the left as one went on into the dining room. A swinging door sepa-rated the dining room and the kitchen.

Because in the early 1800s a lot of the heating of the house was done by fireplaces, there was a fireplace in the dining room and room enough for three good-sized tables and an early American sideboard. A door led into the hallway. On the other side of the hall, the door led into the parlor. All of the rooms had large windows leading from the floor level to six or seven feet toward the ceilings. The ceilings were eleven-feet high on the first floor. All of the windows had interior shutters, which could be opened either by folding the right-side shutter and pushing it back toward the side of the window or doing the same with the left side. These shutters also contained parallel slanted slides, which could be folded up or folded down in such a way that there was a measure of control of the flow of air or light that came in from the outside.

Since the parlor had also been part of an independent apartment, there was a bathroom in back of the parlor. Then there was a series of large rooms with fireplaces, one of which became our bedroom. In the back of our bedroom, there was a smaller room that became Art's office. We hired one woman, Loretta, to help with changing the beds and cleaning the rooms as people left. Art helped with that. He also worked in the dining room in getting people seated and explaining how our breakfast worked for people who were there overnight or for a weekend or several days. We put air-conditioning units in each apartment and installed a furnace in the basement, which would supply heat to the entire building.

At times we had as many as thirty to thirty-five people staying there. I did all of the cooking. This meant that I was in the kitchen most of the day. Some mornings, I would have to get up very early because people would want their breakfast early. However, I refused to get up any earlier than four o'clock in the morning. When we had hunting season, the hunters would want to get up very early and go out to where they were going to shoot turkeys or deer, even though they couldn't start shooting until a particular time when the sun came up. So sometimes, they would leave without eating breakfast.

I served more than the sweet roll, coffee, and juice that many places served for breakfast. I tried to serve a breakfast that would be very satisfying to people. For example, I had a cheese soufflé, which was made the afternoon before, and would serve six to eight people. The recipe was one pound of bulk sausage, two slices of bread (cubed), one cup of sharp cheddar, six eggs, two cups of milk, half a teaspoon of salt, half a teaspoon of dry mustard, and seven drops of Tabasco and Salad Supreme seasoning. This is the seasoning that is put out by McCormick and can be used in many ways. I cooked the sausage and drained it, cubed the bread, removing the crust, and then spread the bread cubes in the bottom of a 10 × 10 or 12 × 8 baking dish. I topped it with the sausage and the cheese and then combined the eggs, milk, and seasoning and poured it over all of that. Then I covered it and refrigerated it overnight. I baked it at 350 degrees for forty-five minutes uncovered. At times, I tried a mixture of cheeses if I did not have enough cheddar. I tried Swiss and Gruyere cheese and that was very good. I experimented with this in various ways but it was a very good dish and people would help themselves. What I tried to do was put the breakfast in the dining room. I made a couple of pots of perked coffee and had hot tea and orange juice. All of this was in the dining room. When people came down for breakfast, they would help themselves. If I didn't have cheese soufflé and had only a couple of people, I might give them bacon and eggs or something of that type. I also had pancakes or French toast at times. I had a complete breakfast menu.

I used recipes from a cookbook called The Breakfast Book written by Marion Cunningham and printed in 1987 by Alfred A. Knopf. It had lots of recipes that made good dishes to serve. There was a glazed cinnamon roll, which made two dozen round cinnamon rolls, and it was excellent. It could be baked the day before and then heated that morning. I made bread almost every day and found good use for that large structure I had built in the middle of the kitchen. I moved my mother from her house in town down to an apartment in McMechen House. This made my time a little easier to manage because she would be very close and I would be able to keep an eye on her. At this time, she was in her mid to upper 90s but still going strong and doing very well.

After ten years of being constantly in the kitchen and on call from early in the morning until late in the evening, I said I had had enough and so we closed McMechen House and sold it personally to a couple who thought they would carry on.

Years before that, we had bought a plot of five acres of land near the golf course and it was right on the river. We decided to build a house up there and spent the next year or so looking at places and deciding exactly where to build the house. There was a nice, round hill on our property that looked down over the field to the river, and that was where we decided to build.

Yard of the McMechen House in Moorefield, WV

Evelyn in the kitchen of McMechen House

Chapter Seven

Impact of War

In the late 30s and 40s, the world was upset with war and rumors of war. This affected the lives of young people who were just graduating from high school and getting ready to go to college. This atmosphere affected all of our lives, particularly of the men who were a part of my life then or who I met later and found that they had been affected by war.

In this chapter I shall consider what happened to the following young men; my brother, Merle Lee Wilson, will be the first one. Next will be Merle Wilson Fallon, my son, followed by James Fallon, my son's father, followed by Arthur Valotto, and then Fenton Babcock.

Merle Lee Wilson

Merle Lee Wilson was my brother. My father was convinced that he could get a job if he went down to Richmond, Virginia. There was a lot of construction going on there, and he thought that he would be able to get a job and take us down to Richmond. We went with him and stayed in a rooming house for a while, then we rented a house up on Church Hill. We were there for a good number of months.

Merle and I had been talking and he was very upset at the idea that he would have his senior year of high school in a big school where he didn't know anyone. So we decided that maybe he should join the US Marines and I would try to join the U.S. Army because, at that time, women were becoming a part of the armed services. If I didn't succeed in that because of my age, or for some reason they wouldn't take me, then I would marry a man whom we had met at the rooming house. He had visited us and had been quite attentive to me. He was going to the Officers Candidate School (OCS), and on weekends, he would come up to the rooming house. We would go to movies or down to the park to walk and he seemed to find me very attractive.

So, Merle and I made our pact that he would join the marines and I would either join a branch of the services or, if that didn't work out, then I would marry Jimmy. In that way, we would be our own bosses without our father having any control over us.

Merle did join the marines without our father being aware that he was going to do that until the deed was done. Then I talked with several of the services and I was discouraged by all of them from joining. Merle had been shipped back to California to be shipped elsewhere in the late fall of 1942. My mother received this letter dated December 28:

Dear Mrs. Wilson,

A mother of one of our boys came to see me yesterday and said if someone would just tell her about her boy, so I thought I would write to you and tell you that my daughter brought your boy home with her from San Diego on Christmas Eve. He is such a nice boy. You can well be proud of him. Frances was on her way home for Christmas. These two boys were on their way to Los Angeles. It was raining so she picked them up. The other boy was Private Francis Hayes from New York. We were so glad to have them for Christmas breakfast. They would not stay for dinner. I must tell you, you know out here at night we do not stop when we see a car parked by the roadside. But Merle insisted that Frances stop so she did and there was a father, mother, and two babies in an open car and it was raining. So the boys got in the back of her little car and they took the people to the next town. Merle went with the man to find a room for his little family. When they got here, they looked like drowned rats. Merle looked well and seemed happy. My friend has her two only boys in the air corps and I have just one girl, I do not have that worry. She is in the navy training station in San Diego, a librarian.

Very sincerely,
Mrs. Authur Schaller,

Fullerton, California

We heard fairly regularly from Merle during the next few months and then he spent some time in New Zealand. He took part in the Battle of Bougainville, Guadalcanal, and was killed in the Battle of Guam. Mother received a letter dated September 27, 1944, and it stated this:

Dear Mrs. Wilson,

It is with deepest regret and sincere sympathy that I am writing this letter to you providing information regarding the death of your son, the late Private Merle L. Wilson, U.S. Marine Corp Reserves. Your son was killed while engaged in actual combat against organized enemy forces in the Central Pacific and within ten feet of me. He was buried with full military honors at an Army Navy and Marine Corp cemetery. Your son was a fine and loyal Marine, who had he been discharged upon the termination of his services, would have received a character marking of "Excellent." He was well liked by his companions and officers of his organization. All the members of his company join me in expressing to you our deepest regret and heartfelt sympathy in your bereavement and render a final salute to a splendid Marine.

Signed,

Wm M. ROOSEVELT

Major, U.S. Marine Corp Reserves.

My mother also received a letter, written on June 9, 1945, from the Third Service Battalion, Service Troops, Third Marine Division, FMS, from Donald Byrnes, Jr., Second Lieutenant, USMCR:

Effective this date, the Service and Supply Company street forming a circle extending from Salgo Road north of the officer's country running west between the company office and the officers mess, thus circling south around the rear of the officers country then circling back east and joining Salgo Road south of the officers, is hereby designated "Wilson Circle" in honor of Private Merle L. Wilson, USMCR. Private Wilson joined Service and Supply Company on the 26 November, 1942 and from that time until his death he proved himself to be an efficient and excellent worker, and was well liked by the officers and men of his company. Private Wilson died from wounds received in action on the 21 July, 1944 at Guam M.I. by order of Major William E. Cullen.

Another letter dated August 15, 1945:

My Dear Mrs. Wilson,

I am enclosing a photograph of a road within our base camp area, which was recently dedicated to the memory of your son as a mark of the admiration and respect felt for him by his own comrades.

In letters, two of them, by J.R. Noffsinger, Chaplain, U.S. Navy Reserve, he stated this,

We have recently dedicated our new service fleet memorial chapel in honor of the men of the Third Motor Transport Battalion, Third Service Battalion, and Third Reconnaissance Company, who have given their lives in battle by serving with this Division. Your son, Merle, is one of these to whom we have dedicated this chapel.

He went on in another letter to give some information about Merle's death. He said that he made the initial landing on Guam in the engagement in which his outfit was involved at the time. He and two others were wounded the first night by shrapnel fire from the enemy. Immediately, Merle was evacuated to a ship for further medical attention after emergency first aid of the latest type was administered. Because of this emergency care, he did not suffer pain, and soon, a blessed unconsciousness spared him any suffering. He passed on quietly soon after reaching the ship, so I am told, and was returned to the island for interment.

Merle Wilson Fallon

Merle is my only child. Mother and I had been living with my grandfather when the war was over and Jimmie came back from Hawaii. When I realized I was pregnant, I went to Cumberland, Maryland, to a gynecologist. I had been small—weighing about 106 pounds. I gained to about 140 pounds and my doctor said I should have a caesarean section.

Merle was named before he was born. He weighed nine and a half pounds and was an exceptionally good baby. He seldom cried, ate well, and slept. As he grew, we noticed that his eyes were drawn to the center of his nose and an ophthalmologist said that an operation was needed to straighten the eyes. We had that done when Merle was four years old. This operation left him with very little sight in one eye. He has worn glasses since then.

I had met and married Arthur Valotto and we were living in the City of Falls Church. Art was employed by the Fairfax County Public Schools, but the City of Falls Church had their own school system, so Merle was in a different school system than where we were employed. He attended high school at George Mason High School. He was not a good student. He was smart enough but he just didn't care about grades. So, he had not done too well but just well enough to get through and graduate from high school. When he finished high school, we visited several colleges and he decided that he wanted to go to Virginia Tech. This was in the mid-sixties.

Once again, the world was upset with war and rumors of war. The young men in America were called upon to register. Some of our young men went with the United Nations in Korea to help settle a situation there. The registration was being used as a means of determining who to draft for a situation that was developing in Vietnam. Merle was in his third year of college at Virginia Tech, and as long as his grades were good, he would not be liable for drafting by the army, but his grades went down and he was drafted. He went into basic training and as soon as that was over, he was being sent to Vietnam.

I had thought he would not be drafted because of the condition of his eyes. However, that didn't seem to matter and he was drafted into the army and he was sent to Vietnam as a noncombatant designation in a group of men designated combatants. Because of this, he was very much involved in action! When the war ended, Merle decided that he would go back to Virginia Tech. This time, he decided to become a student. He ended with a degree and went on and got a master's degree. The university employed him then and as time passed, he decided he would go on and get a degree in law. I believe he was part of the first graduating class in law at the college. He passed through successfully and got his law degree and decided that he would work for a law firm in the District of Columbia.

While there, he saw the young woman who would become his wife. She was a part of the staff there as a legal secretary. They were married and he decided then to begin his own practice in Warrenton, Virginia. That has now become a law firm that he heads. He and Vickie bought a house in Gainesville, Virginia, and have two daughters. He has ended up with a very satisfying life. There are times when individuals within an army can benefit from the experience.

When Merle came back from Vietnam, he was discharged from the army but he had to wear his uniform in order to fly free on standby. His uniform had two rows of ribbons so people knew he was a Vietnam veteran. When he was changing planes in Chicago, a young man with long hair and a beard spit upon Merle to show his dissatisfaction with that war. There is no doubt about the fact that war is hell!

James Fallon

Jimmy had been born in Brooklyn, New York, of parents who were Irish immigrants. He had a brother and a sister and his mother unexpectedly died. His father put all three children into an orphanage. When Jimmy became old enough to join the army, he left the orphanage and joined up. When war was declared in 1942, he was stationed in Alaska. He was a very bright man, and although he had never completed his high school work, he was exceptionally well read and knowledgeable about affairs in the world. At that time, the armed forces were looking for officers, and so Jimmy took a test, which showed his intelligence and his knowledge and he was immediately put in the OCS (Officer Training School). This was in Virginia and it was close to Richmond. On weekends, he would come into Richmond to get away and relax. He was at the same rooming house that my father had taken us and I got to know Jimmy as we ate meals there. He began to visit our apartment and walk with Merle and me as we explored part of Richmond. We didn't go too far from where we were staying but we were getting knowledgeable about the city. When my father moved us into a house on Church Hill, Jimmy visited us there. About that time he received his commission, and he was shipped out to California. He eventually was stationed in Hawaii and he was stationed there for the entire war. The impact of war on his life was positive, because he bettered his education and his prospect of having more jobs available to him after the war.

Arthur Valotto

Art was born in Morgantown, West Virginia, and was the youngest of three children. When the war began, he enlisted in the navy and was eventually assigned to the aircraft carrier USS Franklin. The Franklin was a part of a large group gathered in the South Pacific to attack Japan. He had been on duty all night and was very tired. Instead of going to breakfast, he decided to go back to his bunk and get some rest. Suddenly, a single enemy plane made a low run on the ship and dropped two 250 kilogram bombs, which pierced the deck and set off a chain reaction of the fuel and weaponry that had been placed there ready for fighting. Big Ben was sadly hit. More than 798 young men were killed, with around 487 wounded. The carrier was burning, but because of the heroic effort of the USS Santa Fe, which came close enough to have the wounded transferred to them, they also rescued sailors who had been literally blown off the Franklin into the sea. Big Ben managed to regain power and went to Pearl Harbor. They then continued on to the Brooklyn Navy Yard to be repaired and it was withdrawn for the rest of the war.

Art ended up in a hospital where he spent some time before he was able to return to his home in Morgantown. He did not tell me any of this; I had no idea what had happened to him during the war. This came out here in Winchester, Virginia, because he and a man who had been one of the pilots on the Franklin were eating in the café and recognized each other. John Johnson was a former pilot and he became an admiral before the close of the war. He and Art spent many hours sharing and talking with each other. When a book called The Inferno by Joseph A. Springer was published, I was notified of this by people who had been on the USS Franklin. I immediately sent for one of the books and learned what had happened to him during the war. He never spoke of it and I had no idea what he had gone through.

This experience during the war affected Art for the rest of his life. He went on to get a master's degree and became an assistant principal in a large high school in Fairfax County, Virginia. He spent a lot of time with young people. He would go to work at five or six o'clock in the morning and arrive home after midnight. He was a compulsive worker. This followed through for the rest of his life.

There are several men in the little village where we live in Westminster-Canterbury who were part of that same battle and they eventually found each other. David Greene, who will work with the pictures for our book, was also part of that battle. As Art neared the end of his life, he had been fighting for two years to stay alive and had gone far beyond what his doctor had predicted he would be able to do. As he lay on his death bed, Fenton went to see him and Art recognized Fenton and gestured with his hand. So Fenton took his hand and they clasped hands for a minute or two. When Fenton left then, it was within two or three minutes that Art was gone.

Fenton Babcock

Fenton was among the group of young men who joined up toward the end of World War II and he was a part of the large battle there in the South Pacific.

Early in April 1945, Fenton was serving as a member of the Beach Party on board his attack transport USS Menifee (APA-202). He was preparing to go ashore with the 2,000 marines that the ship had on board on Green Beach Two at Okinawa. This was in preparation for the ultimate attack by the United States on the Japanese homeland. Since he was expecting to be off the ship for a day or two at least, his assignment that morning on board was as a loader for a five-inch gun on the fantail of the ship. Cradling a sixty pound, black powder charge for the antiaircraft gun, he and his shipmates stood frozen to the deck as a kamikaze Japanese suicide dive bomber called a Hamp suddenly broke through the picket line of destroyers protecting the convoy in which the Menifee was sailing and came directly toward his ship.

He and his shipmates concluded that the plane would make a direct hit! There was no way he could miss the ship! The Menifee was zigzagging as the rest of the convoy was, and as the Japanese plane suddenly tried to correct its course, its wing got caught in the water and it crashed right beside the stern of the ship. Since the stern of the Menifee had three antiaircraft positions that were heavily armed with ammunition, they all reached the same conclusion that had that plane hit, the stern of the ship probably would have been blown open and the ship almost certainly would have gone down with all of its 2,000 marines on board.

This sickening thought, however, was relieved by the fate of the Japanese plane failing to make this attack complete. The 500-man crew was very much alerted to the dangers around them. They knew that the large U.S. flotilla of aircraft carriers was in the process of attacking the air bases on the Japanese homeland that were launching the kamikazes, which were trying to turn back the invasion forces.

Included in that group of aircraft carriers was the USS Franklin, which had already suffered from a kamikaze attack in the months before. Now it was returning after the direct attack on these airfields and was heading toward the wider sea. The ship's antiaircraft defenses had been relieved to the extent that some of the crew were being allowed to finally get some food. Among them was Arthur Valotto, who started to join the long chow line with several hundred members of the crew but then decided that he was too tired to remain there and turned and went to his sleeping quarters below the hangar deck.

It was a matter of minutes after that that a Japanese dive bomber suddenly broke through the high cloud cover and dived straight for the Franklin. It's two 500-pound bombs both struck directly and broke through the flight deck, down into the hangar deck below. The explosions among the aircraft that were in the hangar deck turned the area almost instantly into a total inferno. That word is the title of a very important documentary book, giving a direct account of what happened by members of the Franklin crew. All of the several hundred men standing in the chow line were killed instantly. Their charred bodies and body parts were all that remained after the attack was over. The burning aircraft fuel, and the exploding ammunition from the various gun places on the planes that were in the hangar deck, and on the flight deck, created a scene observed by nearby aircraft carriers and other ships.

Art Valotto and many of his shipmates who were below deck found that they were trapped there because of the intensive heat that had buckled many of the hatchways! The smoke was so bad that they could not see their way out of their quarters.

The defensive efforts being taken and other problems aboard had caused the ship, by this time, to be listing badly. Those below decks were at great risk. Finally, as a result of heroic efforts by members of the crew, almost certainly involving Art Valotto directly, the ship limped out of the attack area. He survived and participated directly in the efforts to keep his ship afloat by controlling all of the fires created by the exploding of ammunitions.

It was probably at this time, approximately, that crew members on other ships saw the USS Franklin passing by with its fire hoses trailing in the water. Many concluded that the ship was not going to survive. Fenton and his crew members on the USS Menifee stood at the rail and saluted the heroic ship as she went by. That was a scene reenacted later in a way that seemed to be almost fated from the beginning.

At the end of the war, Fenton returned home and decided to go to Yale University where his father had graduated, class of 1907. Fenton spent nine years there and came out with a doctorate in international studies. He joined the CIA and worked there for over fifty years before he suffered two strokes and lost his eyesight. This, of course, ended his connection with the CIA.

Art and I had been friends with Fenton and his wife, Haya. We had helped Fenton and his daughter, Ann, as much as we could during the period when Haya became critically ill and died. At that time, Fenton and Haya were living in a small apartment in assisted living because Haya needed much assistance from the nursing staff, and in that section of the building, they were able to get that. Following her death, Fenton stayed in assisted living because by that time, he had lost his sight and he needed assistance from the nursing staff also.

Art had also died and I gave Fenton as much help as I could as he settled in to learn to cope with things alone.

Chapter Eight

<u>Animals in My Life</u>

I have always loved animals, dogs, cats, any type of animals, and I have been fortunate to have had in my personal life both dogs and cats. My first dog was given to me when I was about four years old by the veterinarian who lived across the street from us in Moorefield. This was a small puppy that was part bulldog and part several other breeds. She became a lovely dog but her loyalty was given to my older brother, Wayne. She used to follow him around. I cannot recall all of the dogs and cats that I have had, but some stand out in my memory more than others.

I think my first cat was a coal-black cat that I called Ink Spot or Inky. I used to carry her around on my shoulders. I also had another cat that was as gold as he could be and he used to walk with his tail straight up in the air and I called him Tom Tail-in-the-air. A cat that lives in my memory and is perhaps the only cat that I failed with was April. I had to give up April, not because I wanted to but because it was necessary. April was a Siamese cat and I got her from the Siamese cat center. She had been born in Ohio and run away. She was adopted by somebody in Florida and had run away. She had a reputation as being an escape artist cat. When I went to the Siamese control center, they had sixty cats that were up for adoption. In order to visit that center, I needed to fill out a form in which I expressed my desire to do that and I was required to give three references of people they could contact to make sure I was a person who would be a good owner of a cat. They contacted each of the three people that I had put down on that paper, and then they told me that I could come out to the center to visit. When I got there, I found that it was a large building that had two floors and many cats that needed homes.

I went in the building where there were two people who were full-time staff to take care of the cats. They were there to help with adoption if that was what you decided you wanted to do. There were sixty cats on the two floors, some small kittens and some very old cats. There was one cat that was in a cage but most of the cats were wandering around on the two floors. They had plenty of room for exercise and play. I asked about the cat that was in the cage and the reply was that every time she was let out of the cage, she caused a fight. I said that's the cat I want. And so, we started the adoption proceedings. They contacted my veterinarian and after a short length of time, I was told that I could have the cat that I had wanted—April was her name.

She was a purebred Siamese, had been born in Ohio and ended up down in Florida and then eventually came to Virginia. I live in a senior village, designed for senior citizens. It is called Shenandoah Valley Westminster-Canterbury and I had come to this village particularly because I was allowed to have animals. I had visited eight different places and SVWC was the only place that allowed a resident to keep a cat or a dog. So, this is where I decided to settle. My husband Art and I had moved in here and I had immediately started looking for a place where I could get a dog or a cat. I found the cat center for Siamese cats and had ended up adopting April from there. I had to sign a paper that she would be a house cat and not be allowed to go outside. That suited me fine. And for six or seven years it suited April. Art had died and April became my full-time companion.

Among the couples that Art and I had particularly enjoyed was Haya, a German woman who had married a man in the CIA. They had a cat and understood cats. April liked Haya and Fenton and when they stopped by, she would go and greet them and often end up on Fenton's lap. April had been an escape artist and every time there was a door opened, she would rush out. She was a very fast cat. She liked other people, however, and would let someone pick her up and she was brought back to her home.

After Haya's death and then Art's death, Fenton and I began to feel a close friendship and he visited here and ate meals here and April liked that, as she liked him. She would stretch out on his knee and feel very much at home. Eventually, we decided that we would spend all of our time together and get married. So he got ready to move in here and April liked that, too. However, there was a problem, because every time the door opened, out she would go. So I became more and more alert to preventing that.

I had been told that you could not train a cat. I saw that she was such a smart cat and I could not see why she couldn't be trained. So I started to train her to stay away from doors. Fenton had moved in here after we were married and she loved that, but every time she would go close to a door, I would be after her. I was feeling pretty good about training her because she was getting trained. I thought what a smart cat she was. However, one Saturday morning, about 5 a.m., she came over to where I was sleeping and bit me on the hand and then went down to my foot and bit me on the foot through the covers and went down into my ankle. I naturally screamed and had a fit that she would do that! After things had settled down, Fenton and I met with our veterinarian and he pointed out that this was not normal actions for a cat and when that happens, it was a warning that she would end up by putting me in the hospital! It was evidently because I was trying to train her and she did not want to be trained.

I called the Siamese control center and they sent someone to get her. That was the end of my relationship with that wonderful cat! Never again will I try to train a cat.

Three dogs live in my memory and I had them when we were in Manassas, when my son Merle brought in two wire-haired terriers that he and his first wife had gotten. They were in the process of breaking up their marriage and they did not want the dogs and so they brought them to me. I had already gotten a small puppy of the breed called Great Pyrenees and she was just a pup at that time. She and the two dogs that Merle had brought got along beautifully most of the time.

We had a large swimming pool, 20 × 40 feet, which had a diving board. Merle would often go up on the diving board and jump off. He would be followed by the two wire-haired terriers; they loved the water—the Great Pyrenees did not. We called the Great Pyrenees

Sunny because she was white and quite a beautiful dog. We had about an acre and a half with that house and the swimming pool was placed at the back of the house. Around the swimming pool, there was a seven-foot high fence with a gate that opened to one of the yards. The large yard was divided into two parts; there was the part that came out from the swimming pool, and beyond that, the whole lower end of the lot was fenced. There was a division between the swimming pool yard and the large yard in back.

While Sunny had not been cross, we had no idea that she would in any way protect us. But one day, we were out in the backyard and did not hear UPS deliver a package. She could hear us talking out in back and so she decided to come around and deliver the package to us personally. I think she wanted to see what the backyard looked like. So she came around and opened the gate leading into the smaller fenced-in yard. At that time, Sunny came out and saw her and ran over and bit her. This caused a lot of consternation on all of our parts. She was very nice about this and I insisted that she go to the hospital and get a shot and get the bite tended to. She did so and we heard nothing more about that. There was no pressing of any charges. However, we knew that Sunny would be a very protective dog.

Another instance where Sunny showed her protectiveness was in the car. I had the dogs in the car with me, and for some reason, Parish started acting peculiarly. Sunny snapped at Parish. She snapped back and they ended up in a fight in the backseat of the car. I got in the middle of that fight in order to stop it and ended up with seven bites. I was in the hospital that night, getting my bites taken care of.

This was during the period of time when I was traveling back and forth to Moorefield to take care of my elderly relatives. So, Art and I decided that we should sell the house in Manassas and move to Moorefield. We bought a large old house in Moorefield which had thirty rooms and decided to open a bed and breakfast. It was there that I did all of the cooking and was a very busy person. We had had a small yard at the back of McMechen House, fenced-in for the dogs. Art liked to take a long walk every morning or some time during the day and he would usually take Sunny with him.

While we lived in that large house in Moorefield and ran the bed and breakfast, one Sunday morning, a small dog was hit by a car in front of our house. I immediately went out and gathered the little dog up and took him into our back porch. He was a dog of many breeds. He had very short legs and a fat little body and became one of our nicest pets. That day, we got our vet to come into his office and Dr. Morris took care of him and kept him over night. The next day, I picked him up and brought him into McMechen House and nursed him through the recovery period. I named him after the veterinarian, calling him Morris.

These were but a few of the pets that I have had over my lifetime. All of them were wonderful animals and some of them came from an unknown background but became great pets and I loved them dearly. I do not have a dog or a cat now, but one of the reasons we moved to Westminster-Canterbury was because we were able to have a pet! I see all sorts of dogs and cats in SVWC. Some are big dogs and some are little dogs. Some of their owners live in houses such as we do and some of them live in apartments. Everyone seems to accept the animals and speak to them in a very caring way when they see them.

Some of the dogs become visiting dogs and go into various parts of the buildings to visit people who may be there, such as in the assisted living quarters. We have one particular dog called Rowdie, a big black dog who takes his master for a walk almost every day. Rowdie is very old, but he still loves to go into the driveway, pick up the newspaper, and drop it at the door.

A cat named Annie lives in an apartment in one of the buildings on the fourth floor. She likes to sit in the doorway of her home and many people stop to talk with her and pet her as they pass. Occasionally, she will go down the hall for a few steps but not very far.

As I mentioned in my earlier writing, when Art and I were looking for a life care community we wanted to join, we visited seven or eight different places in Pennsylvania, Delaware, Virginia, West Virginia, and Maryland. This was the only place where animals were allowed. We have lots of them living here. They fit in beautifully and become known to many residents. It was wonderful to discover that there was a place where you could live and take your animals, regardless of how old you are. People here are interested in animals and our small newspaper occasionally has a page of photographs of pets of the people who live here.

Evelyn with kitty

Brother Merle when he joined the Marines

Evelyn with her dog

Chapter Nine

<u>Watching Myself Age</u>

Although I was 9.8 lbs when I was born, as I grew I became slender and was small boned and had hair that had a tendency to wave around my face. I was introduced to the dentist quite early and he was our friend and not a doctor to me, so I had care on my teeth at an early age. There was a period when I was around three years old that I do not remember, but have been told by my mother that I lost my ability to walk and they blame the girl who had been hired to take me for walks for walking me too far. I overcame that problem and have no memory of it at all.

My earliest memory was around the age of three and a half or four, when I remember distinctly the sound of a small cricket that was on our stairway, and as I went up to bed each night, I would hear that cricket until I reached a certain point on the stairway and then it would become silent.

Most of my early memories are of living in the new house that my father had built, and that involved playing out in the yard with Merle and two neighborhood boys, Woog and Bill. Of course, my most constant companion was Merle, and we were very close. He was a year older than I. When we moved into the new house; it had been built adjacent to my maternal grandparents, and their house became almost the same as my house. I was very close to them and spent a lot of time over there, eating meals or just sprawling on the floor and reading the comics.

I do not remember learning to read; it seems to me I always had that ability. My brother Merle had the same ability, so we shared the newspaper and enjoyed keeping up with certain items, such as the comics.

My first animal that I remember was given to me when I was about four years old by the veterinarian who lived across the street. It was a small puppy that had been just a few weeks old and I immediately named her Tippy. As she grew, she attached herself to my older brother, Wayne, so she was not my dog; she was Wayne's dog. However, she was in the house and I loved her and we got along very well together. I do not remember the first cat; I have just always had cats. So animals were very much a part of my early world. My closest playmate was my brother Merle, and we were together all the time. We played together along with Woog and Bill, who were living next door. So I played a lot of boy games. I had dolls, a baby buggy, and dishes, and I didn't play with any of those.

When I was eleven years old, one day, Merle and I were playing in the house and I went to one of the baskets for soiled clothes that had a lid on it. I was hiding from him as I climbed in that clothes basket and pulled the lid down and let him hunt for me. That was fine, but when I got out I had blood all over myself and I didn't know what in the world had happened. I screamed for my mother who came and that was when she told me about the monthly period that women have. She had given no indication or preparation for that and I will never forget my feeling when I realized what had happened, that I was in the process of becoming a woman.

These early years were very happy. I joined the choir at the church, as did Merle. We enjoyed singing and we also had some singing groups at the house with mother playing the piano. My brother Wayne, Merle, and later, Wayne's wife, all made a singing group and we enjoyed that.

Physically, I remained slender and not too tall. I was fairly average height. I was over five feet when I got into my teens. I ended up at 5' 4" and weighing about 106 lbs. when I was eighteen. I was eighteen when my family went to Richmond for about a year. During these late-teen years, a lot of youngsters had very bumpy skin on their faces with skin eruptions. I did not. My skin just remained almost as it was when I was a young child. During these late-teen years, I remained slender and I was interested in almost everything going on around me. I was curious about so many things that I saw. I always pursued that curiosity until I was satisfied and went on to another subject, or another area. I became a part of a group of girls with four to six of us doing things together. I enjoyed school and enjoyed learning about new things; therefore, the science and biology classes were very interesting to me.

During these years, I wore my hair at varied lengths, going from a short cut with bangs to letting it grow until it was way down on my shoulders. Sometimes, I would wear it up in a ponytail or wear it held back by combs. I had nice, abundant hair which was brown. I always envied my older brother's red hair or Merle's golden hair, and along came Evelyn who managed to get brown hair. This, I felt, was not very fair.

During the late-teen years, I became very interested in my fingernails and that was when I really began trying to shape them the way I wanted them and began to paint my nails with varied colors. My father objected to this but didn't forbid me from doing it.

I was eighteen at the time of the war and it was during that time that my brother Merle and I made a pact that he would join one of the armed services and that I would marry a man who we had met at a boardinghouse in Richmond. That man's name was James Fallon and I married him at eighteen in order to get away from my father's dictatorial manner. So at eighteen, I became my own boss, so to speak, and could make my own decisions and do whatever I had money to do. As the wife of an army officer, I had a monthly income. Jimmie was over in Hawaii. Mother and I were living with my grandfather in his big house in Moorefield, West Virginia. My father was down in Richmond working. Mother and I felt very good because we were our own bosses and I became self-confident and developed an ability to manage.

My grandfather did not like my father, although there were times when the two of them lived together in the same house and there was never anything overtly there that they did not get along, but they really stayed away from each other as much as possible. So it was at this time that I began to educate myself in various things that really interested me and that was the way I took my courses at the beginning.

When the war ended and Jimmie came home, we immediately decided to further our education and we went to a junior college connected to West Virginia University and we started getting our degrees. This was a very busy time in my life because I was interested in getting more courses at a college or university, I had a young son, I had a husband who was also going to school, so we were busy all the time and not aware of time passing.

I was very fortunate that I stayed slender after my child was born. I regained my slender stature and I wore the same clothes for several years and it didn't bother me at all. I developed a lot of self-confidence and the ability to manage the situation that I happened to be in that I wanted to manage. And I did not try to manage those situations that I didn't care about or where I had only a non-managerial responsibility. In the early 1950s, I had become interested in how children learn to read, and in order to satisfy my curiosity, I started going to school at George Washington University where they had courses in learning to read. In the late 1950s, I received my master's degree and began working with some individuals in their reading clinic. This meant going over into D.C. on Saturdays and in the late evening during the week. During the early 1960s, the nation as a whole began looking and talking about the education of a young child. Congress set up the Head Start program in various places.

Art and I found an old farmhouse in Manassas, which had been restored and had a large 20 × 40 foot swimming pool in its backyard, so we were very pleased with it. We had three dogs and two cats. Art was involved with the Lions Club and I took over the care of our big yard. We had several acres, which were at the edge of Manassas. I was not conscious of being tired at any time and I mowed that lawn by a push mower. I also did a lot of entertaining during the spring, summer, and fall.

In my late thirties, I began to bleed a lot during my monthly periods, and at the age of thirty-five, I had a hysterectomy and began taking estrogen. The doctor never took me off that estrogen until finally I took myself off at age seventy.

At age forty, I had a lot of trouble with my thyroid and they removed a large part of my thyroid gland; this meant that I needed to take a supplement for the rest of my life. I developed high blood pressure, and I was put on medicine for that, which I continue to take. I was also put on Detrol.

One of the worst things that happened was that I had a severe fall, face forward on concrete, into a group of people. I had no idea that I was going to fall. I did not trip or stumble; I just fell face forward. That happened here at Westminster-Canterbury in one of the parking lots. Someone immediately called for the nurse from the clinic, who got me back to my home and on the bed and then doctored all of the scrapes and bruises that I had. I broke three of my front teeth; the crown of my nose was badly scraped, but it did not break. There seems to be no reason for the fall so the hypothesis is that it was due to an inner ear malfunction.

I am now eighty-six, and although I can tell I am not as strong as I was at fifty, I think that I do fairly well. I work out in our fitness room three times a week for thirty minutes at a time, and I am still doing the fitness exercises that Art designed for me when we first moved here. He had an advanced degree in that and he knew what he was doing. It has kept me fairly trim and fairly agile, although my weak area is my legs. They were weak when I was three years old and they are still weak when I was eighty-five years old, but I work at keeping them going. I do a lot of exercises in the fitness room connected with leg development and movement. My goal is to retain the ability to walk and get around and go where I want to go without being in a wheelchair. I am hoping that exercising will help me do that.

Sexually, I am still a very responsive person; I always was and I don't believe that my responsiveness has declined much with age. My hair was always fairly heavy, it was rather fine, and it does have a tendency to wave if it is treated correctly. I still do that with nice shampoo under the shower and then I let it dry, and when it is dry, I take a hot brush and brush it in sections, and when I finish, it oftentimes is in waves. It is down to my shoulders and I wear it up. Very seldom do I wear it down anymore. It is not completely grey but it is turning that way. My muscles are beginning to relax in spite of all the exercising and walking that I do. I find that I am not able to walk as much. I would rather it not be hot, even at seven and eight o'clock in the morning. Heat affects me so that I do not walk and that is going to count against me eventually. The muscles in my face are relaxing.

I notice this particularly in the wedding picture of Fenton and myself, and I felt there must be some mistake. But I have gradually realized that the mistake that I was making was that I felt my face was still as taut as it used to be, and it is not. The muscles are relaxing and my face looks fuller. The muscles in my abdomen are relaxing and I try very hard to keep my exercises going to so that I will not have a large stomach as so many older people do.

I noticed that I do not have as many interests as I used to have. I was always very curious about everything, from the animal world up to the human world. But that curiosity is not as great anymore. I am still curious about the animal world. One of the reasons I came to SVWC was because they allowed us to have animals. We can have dogs or cats. My chapter on animals explains why we have gradually cut down and we do not have an animal anymore—no dog, no cat. I know my memory is not as good as it used to be, but I am fortunate to be married to a man who has an excellent memory. Fenton supplies me with information that I need when I don't remember it. I would be taking courses in various things. One reason I wanted to come to Winchester is because there is a university here. I have gone to school all my life and would do so now, but I don't have the time. There are courses available at Shenandoah University and they often have a course held right here at SVWC, but I have been too busy to find out what is being held each semester.

My confidence in driving the car is lessening. At one time, I was able to go any place with no problem, but now I am beginning to be aware that I am not really sure how to get to various places even though I have been there before. My memory in remembering turns and so on is not as great. This has affected my confidence in driving.

I have not maintained contact with my group of friends from high school. We maintained contact for a good many years, but I do not have the time or interest to write letters and I do not care to talk on the telephone. And I don't drive there very often, so gradually over the years, the contact has dropped. This past year I didn't even get to send out Christmas cards because of things that were happening in my life here. So, those contacts are gradually dropping off. I am not one to talk on the telephone for long periods of time. That is not the way I prefer to maintain contact.

Our life here is quiet and we are busy from the time we get up in the morning until we go to bed at night. I couldn't work too much more into a day than my day has at the present time. Fenton and I enjoy talking. We can sit and talk for long periods of time and not even realize that time is passing. This is very interesting to me and I enjoy that type of contact with him.

He has a daughter and I have a son and they feel as if they have found a brother and a sister. They come to see us periodically to spend several hours in the evening. Both of them are seriously employed in business affairs but they do come and see us, and we, as a family, are fairly close.

Fenton's Memoirs

Chapter Ten

My Beneficial Upbringing

The ancestry of my father, Thorpe Babcock, dates back to 1604, when James Babcock arrived from Wyveanho, England. This Babcock strain tended to stay in New England. My father grew up in Quincy, Massachusetts, and ultimately East Milton. The revolution musket that had been used by Captain William Babcock was well preserved by my father along with the beautiful original Aaron Willard grandfather's clock that he had inherited.

From the family house on President's Hill, my father studied in local high school and then worked in the yacht design business during his vacations to raise money for his college training at Yale University in New Haven, Connecticut. Graduating in 1907 as a law student, he had a record of active participation in sports, including baseball, swimming, and rowing with the Yale Crew. I must note that he left Yale with the nickname of "Big Chief Bleeding Heart." With several classmates, he headed West upon graduation to find gold in Alaska and had, of course, disappointment in that regard. Instead, he entered into the State of Washington's lumber business. Starting from the very bottom rung, he and his friends stacked lumber and then finally worked into the management stream.

After serving for several years as the secretary of the West Coast Lumberman's Association, he became the manager of a fairly large mill in Hoquiam, Washington. That is where my life began as a youngster in 1926. Through my father's own published memoir entitled Broke at Forty-five, I learned of the early years when his mill burned to the ground during the First World War. It was rapidly rebuilt with government assistance in order to continue its production of the critical spruce wood that was used in the making of airplanes. That same type of wood had been used in the manufacture of the Spirit of St. Louis, the plane flown by Colonel Lindbergh across the Atlantic in 1926. It was his 1927 flight to the State of Washington to thank some of the lumber people for the origin of that wood brings my first memory as a youngster. Although all others deny the possibility of my memory, I swear it occurred in a baby carriage on one bright day, when Colonel Lindbergh flew over and dipped his wings to the local town. Looking up from my baby carriage past the standing adults around me, I was privileged to see that black dot move across the sky!

My family, of course, made clear to me the pleasant upbringing I had had as a baby between ages one and three in the home of the mill manager, right on the water there, with nannies to help to take care of two children. I learned also of the heartrending loss of the firstborn son in the family, Thorpe Babcock, Jr., and then became actually aware of the changes when in 1929, the family had to pull up its stakes and head to California to start a whole new life.

My father's book was well read in lumbering circles, but for me, it brought the treasured story about how he and my mother met. Traveling together by chance on the ferry boat Chipawah near Seattle, he had spotted the most beautiful girl he had ever seen. Being the "Big Chief" he was, he gave a fifty cent piece to the maitre d' in the dining room to bring the young lady and her escort to his table. By 1911, he was married to her in a small town lumber area, and she had turned her back on her life in Nebraska and New York City. Her father, Louie Spencer, had tragically lost his life at a train station in trying to save a mother and small child, and was himself hit by a very heavy baggage cart and killed. This ended his career as a concert level pianist. My mother then went east to live with her aunt, Eleanor White, in New York City, at 59th Street in Central Park South. There she entered the life of piano study at Carnegie Hall and accompanying her aunt to the Metropolitan Museum where her aunt was a certified copier. From there, she went on to the Chicago Art Institute for her own training as an artist.

My conscious life began at the height of The Great Depression with our family arriving in Southern California, first in Los Angeles and then in the smaller city of Pasadena. While occupying a very large rental house in Pasadena, I had my first exposure to the extremely close relationship between my father and mother. It centered around the illness of my mother, Mabel Spencer Babcock, which was described to me later as life threatening. My memory was that of tremendous concern in the family over the fear on the part of my father that he would soon be left with three children, my sister Dorothy Babcock, my bother Milton Babcock, and myself. We would have a new life as my father had no job and was in a new, strange area. In the words of my father spoken several times over the subsequent years, a miracle happened and my mother's extremely high fever from her illness broke, and she thereafter was a strong and supportive mother and wife that we all came to know and revere.

After exposure to my first severe earthquake, I became conscious of our new life in the delightful bungalow that we acquired in Pasadena on La Loma Road. I began to grow up with the great support and leadership of not just my parents, but my sister and brother also. By hard study and work, my father was able to get a new start in business in real estate and he led our family through that particularly difficult time. Memories still linger of the years when well-dressed men would come to the front door and beg for money or food to sustain their families during the height of The Depression. I also remember the sight of the lines of early Ford motor cars with children hanging out from the back, parking on our street and on their way to Los Angeles through Pasadena, trying to find a new way of life as we were also.

Perhaps my warmest memory of those years was the Sunday afternoon music sessions we had as a family, with my mother playing the piano, my brother the violin, and my sister, father, and I all singing wonderful songs that were particularly popular in those days. "Danny Boy" was certainly one of the frequent songs to be sung, but I know in retrospect it was perhaps the hardest for my mother and father because their first son had been called Laddie Boy, and that loss to them was a great factor in their lives. We knew that it had bound them together in a firm way that had benefited all of us. The many painful steps of my father toward a new career and the wonderful support given to him by our mother, who was literally sewing on her machine his shirts in those days, taught us all a great deal about appreciation for life.

I owe a great deal to my sister and brother for their examples over those years. My sister, six years older, was an effective shepherdess for me. Not only did she properly kid me about my many girlfriends, but she showed great deftness in handling her own contacts with young gentlemen coming to visit her. That circle of young men included John Philips, the man who she married and who has been such a wonderful husband for her ever since. This wonderful family of fine young people lived most of their lives in the State of Oregon.

My relationship with my brother Milton became increasingly close despite the three years separating us, simply because of the many things he taught me, in woodworking, for example, and tennis and boxing. When he and my father built an eighteen-foot sailboat in the backyard, which was enjoyed by all of our family during our annual one month at the beach years later, he taught me a great deal about sailing. Ultimately, he and I, I as the assistant to him as skipper, appeared in the movie Philadelphia Story, when sailing in a star class boat in a group swirling around the barge out in the ocean which was holding the cameramen, all of whom got seasick.

Milton preceded me into the service by joining the merchant marines and as a third engineer on new ships, showed me in one instance, the great loyalty he had to his first love. When his ship was wrecked in heavy seas on the Galapagos Islands, off Latin America, he undertook to swim back to the ship on the request of the captain to obtain the ship's log. Being a strong swimmer, he was able to make the trip and, while on board, obtain also his picture of his lady friend who was then to become his first wife.

Our close, warm, family circle was helped also by a fine cousin named Henry Bray, who was a frequent companion for us youngsters but also was an excellent tennis player who then provided all of us with tennis capability that served us throughout our remaining lives. Standing out most strongly in my memory, though, was my Aunt Corinne, my father's youngest sister, who would come frequently on weekends. She spent many hours with me in a separate room of the small house reading, discussing, and, particularly, teaching me to increase my French language. Above all, she pointed me in the direction of higher education, which I was then to undertake after three years in the service and to make a career for myself in service to the country.

In sum, I was blessed by a life growing up in a then-beautiful town of Pasadena, the home of the annual Rose Parade, with clear skies and before there was so much smog and crowded highways with vehicular traffic. I benefited from a good school system. I followed after my sister and brother and prepared as I planned at that time, to try to be accepted at the naval academy. My own school record included my selection as the middle school class president and the winner of the annual Kiwanis Club award as well as basketball and track and field experience that then helped me at the collegiate level. In retrospect, however, perhaps my greatest disappointment was in myself for not using the piano training given me by my mother to provide her with some beautiful Chopin but having turned rather to boogie-woogie and the type of music that didn't appeal to her or my father.

While my first marriage was not welcomed by my parents, they ultimately came to recognize its strong contribution to my career of fifty years with the Central Intelligence Agency. Following the death of my late wife, I have found in the singing duets with my wonderful current wife some of the old songs, such as those loved by my parents. I am able to think that I am paying tribute to the upbringing they gave me and the example they set of a strong, happy marriage, and the attention and help given by me and my first wife to our outstanding daughter over the years.

This is my assessment of the base experience on a strength of which I was able to stand very fortunately, and proceed well beyond friendship under the philosophy of Ai Chin toward the new life from old that I have.

My father brought to that base development of my character that of a New Englander who had proceeded through difficult family circumstances to obtain the education necessary to move onward and upward in the world of business. He always said to his two sons, my brother and I, that there were just two kinds of men, those who had been able to meet a payroll and those who had not had to meet a payroll. That, of course, was a rather harsh description, but it certainly stayed in my mind for the rest of my years. It meant to me that when I had a responsibility for those working for me, and with me, that this responsibility absolutely had to be fulfilled.

At the same time in bringing up his family, my father displayed a love for poetry that not only to some degree softened his appearance and posture, but it also showed an understanding of a wisdom that there is in much poetry, that which extends far beyond our own normal understanding. My father would walk through the house reciting the poetry that he had obviously learned as perhaps a youngster in New England and which he had retained in his mind throughout his life. Emerson, for example, was one of his favorites, which extends a wide horizon between patriotic-type poetry, which was probably common during the revolutionary years, and the focus on the beauty of nature and the many lessons that nature teaches us daily if we are prepared to address it and focus on it.

My father was a strong father in the family. He was a true leader in the family, but at the same time was a kind and understanding father who took pride in teaching his children as he went along. Among the many lessons taught, perhaps the most important was that of deference toward our mother, and he never let us break out of that pattern and we, hopefully, did not do so. Since I was growing up in The Depression years, my consciousness was of the economic difficulties that were being overcome by our family and the fact that we all had to adjust accordingly.

As those years went by, we saw our father gain in his confidence; regain his confidence as a business person and his preparedness to give as he could provide it to our family the niceties that we then benefited from. The most obvious of that was the annual one-month vacation at the seashore at Balboa Island south of Los Angeles and the wonderful life that was for us as a family.

When I was privileged to accompany my father on a sentimental journey back to the Seattle area, specifically Hoquiam, where his mill had been under his direction and to recapture through his eyes and his memory the life that he and the family had had at that time. When I was with him, he was interviewed by a radio personality in Seattle and I heard again those things that I had heard in snippets over the years about his career and the fact that he had been, indeed, a leader in the field of lumbering and, thereby, had experience in the difficulties and successes that went with that business. Through our conversations on that plane coming and going, I was able to recapture again, through him, the life of country club involvement and his ability as a good golfer to stand out and his ability to be a public speaker at some of the conventions that were held.

He recalled, for example, the day when he and my mother had been hosted by the college club in Seattle as founders of that club. It was very obvious that he fit into that life of the businessman developing and growing up in Seattle, and who then had had to break out of that circle and restart his whole life in a new frontier area of California.

That was the same father who, despite all the difficulties of restarting his professional life, found time on weekends to take us children to see the tar pits in Los Angeles where the bones of prehistoric animals had been found and who would also take us out to the countryside for a game of softball.

When he would come on weekends from his place of business in our home in Pasadena to join us during our vacation in our rented house at the beach, he showed the wonderful ability to relax. We would follow the tradition of walking around Balboa Island in the evening and viewing all the sights and sounds of that wonderfully restful and quite delightful vacation life. This was the same father who on one occasion taught me the very important lesson of deference to workmen whom I had addressed without adequate deference.

When I would ride with him when he was frequently driving back to her own home the African-American lady who came to clean our house and help my mother in taking care of dinner parties, he taught me to show her the highest respect. Mrs. Ruffin showed a work ethic to all of our family and a loyalty that stayed with us all of the succeeding years. In my case, it became an introduction to a warm friendship with the granddaughter, Sheila, who then married and became Mrs. Warren Johnson and who raised a very fine family. That warm friendship has been renewed every year at Christmastime and has resulted in trips to our home in Virginia.

Perhaps the strongest memory of a base building in my life was the Sunday afternoon music sessions that brought the whole family together around the piano. My mother played very well and my brother was good, indeed, on the violin. My father and sister loved to sing, and I also, so we produced warm, enjoyable music based on the grand old selection of those days.

As my father was the leader of the family, our mother was the backbone of our family's daily life. She never shied away from hard work around the house, with all the laundering, cooking, and cleaning that was done regularly by her, only to be supplemented by the visits of Mrs. Ruffin. Washing and ironing for a busy family was a constant strain on my mother, I am convinced of that. I am happy to say that I pitched in to do as much as I could to relieve her of that. When the family graduated from a hand ringer to an automatic one, I remember distinctly that her hand got caught in the ringer and she never flinched from the pain. Later on an occasion, when she was in the hospital at one point and I was accompanying her down one of the hallways, I recall that her hand hit and was caught by a very heavy door at one of the stairways; she again was clearly in severe pain but appeared not to show it to anyone. One other characteristic that stands out in my memory is my mother's love of her garden and her efforts to maintain it as best she could. She went to great lengths to teach me the names of most of the plants in the garden, and I, thereby, had a real desire to garden.

Our home was blessed by a selection of literature that my mother inherited from her father, and she made certain that we would benefit from that in reading, for example, all the works of Dickens. During our annual month at the seashore, she made sure that we all read some books most of the time when we were resting, and she recorded on maps the countries that were addressed in those various works of literature.

Fenton's parents

Fenton's family dog

Babcock family grouping for tennis
Fenton, Sister Dorothy, Brother Milton,
Father Thorpe,Cousin Henry Bray

Chapter Eleven

<u>Living My Heritage through Two First Loves</u>

The first was the undergraduate life at Yale University. The second was falling in love for the first time with a New Englander who showed me and taught me the beauty and the value of small town New England life. Through both of these first two loves, I came to realize and appreciate the lessons I had learned in the last year of my navy service prior to mustering out in mid-April in 1946.

Those lessons came to me when I became a member of a team of helmsman for our ship and began to work toward a position as a quartermaster third class. Our ship was still preparing for the attack on the Japanese homeland so we were still zigzagging in convoy, and as helmsman, one of the strongest lessons was to make sure that the course was being steered straight and narrowly. The officer of the deck on the bridge had no difficulty in observing my facing towards the stern of the ship, whether or not the wake was going straight and narrow, and if it were not, the helmsman was not doing his work properly. In a big ship like ours, 550 feet long with a heavy load of equipment and troops, it took very little to steer improperly by turning the wheel too strongly.

While moving in convoy, the zigzagging was strictly imposed with a chart facing the helmsman, which showed the exact times to the second that a turn was to be made to port or starboard. It was made clear also that that turn was not to be made at all without the command from the officer of the bridge.

The lesson that was to remain with me all my life came at one point when a clock was ticking down and the time for the closely controlled turn was to be required and the officer of the deck was out of reach on the wing of the bridge. I well knew that turning in a convoy was a very trying experience because you have immediately almost the impression that you were going to crash into the next ship, but that, of course, did not occur because of the strictly controlled pattern of turns. In this case, my memory was very clear on this that the time came and it fell to me to make the turn without the command that was required, so I made the turn. Needless to say, the officer came flying to the hatch and flung it open and I could see that he was as white as a sheet when he came to realize that he had missed his call and I had made the turn anyway. He and I for the rest of our time aboard that ship were close friends, each protecting the other and that memory will always be in my mind as one that was to be treated very carefully.

The third lesson that remained in my mind throughout and very effectively in my first two loves of undergraduate life, and my first time falling in love, was that control and care go closely together.

In this case, our ship at some later date came into a busy harbor in the United States. I was at the helm on the flying bridge, out in the fresh air on top of the wheelhouse, and we had a pilot on board to get us into the harbor safely. While the pilot was giving his commands to an assistant who would blow a whistle downward towards the tugboat that was pushing against the ship, I was at the helm giving calls through a speaking tube to the engine room for slight changes to the speed of the ship. Needless to say, my commands were those relayed to me by the captain of our ship and he was standing right beside me. In the case of my memory, which is engraved there forever, the pilot called, "going four," and guess what Fenton the Helmsman did! He turned to the speaking tube and called, "Blow Four." To the horror of our captain, that meant that the main whistle on the ship would be sounded four times, blasting all of our ears and calling attention to all the ships in the harbor that our ship was in a state of disaster. The captain turned instantly toward me and yelled, "Belay that call!" which I then did through the speaking tube. I never knew whether the captain and the pilot got a laugh out of that event, but they certainly never showed it to me.

Having these valuable lessons in my mind for the rest of my life, I was able to enter this new life in New England.

My family provided all of the strength and backup and encouragement that were needed for this new chapter in my life, and I proceeded to New Haven, Connecticut, in the fall of 1946. There I found a whole new world in the campus of Yale University, the gothic style and the whole atmosphere was totally new for me, and it, of course, told me of the life my father had led some forty years before but also the life that went back some 250 years, to the beginning of Yale University and all of the traditions that had ensued in the following years.

As a freshman, I lived in what was called the Old Campus, consisting of a quadrangle of wonderful old dormitories; my dormitory faced right across the Green to the one which my father had occupied. Meals were served at the Commons Building half a block away and the life for me began to revolve around my roommate who was again the source of a lesson for me. He was a graduate from one of the fine private secondary schools in New England. He brought to me the studying habits which I had never learned as a public school product in California. It was only these methods and habits that then helped me get through my undergraduate years at Yale and onward to the five years of graduate work that were to follow.

Having discovered quickly that my prowess as a junior high school team player counted for nothing in trying to qualify for the Yale basketball team, I then turned upon the suggestion of the coach to another sport. Fortunately I chose that of rowing, which my father had engaged in as a Yale student, and it came to be part of my life and it caused me to apply myself as a student in order to survive. This was particularly true because the rowing took place one-half hour away by bus travel and the half-hour returning from the Housatonic River and by the time I got back, study was the one thing I had to do most of all. There was time, however, on weekends, to move around the wonderful little city of New Haven and enjoy the atmosphere; for example, at The Green with the three historic churches and the sounding of their bells, or walking into the neighborhoods and seeing all of the houses of earlier years. In short, I was being bitten by the bug of New England, which I had never experienced before. This effect was not in any way set back by my involvement in boxing at

Yale and I was able to qualify for that team as well as Crew. In both of these sports, I came to apply the lessons that I had learned as a helmsman on my ship prior to leaving the navy, notably the lessons of accuracy, care, and control.

As a student during my sophomore, junior, and senior years at Yale, in one of the residential quadrangular settings with its own dining room and library that can be so beneficial, I found a new life that was highly advantageous. This was particularly because of the system in which Fellows Faculty Members lived or spent much of their time in the small sub college. They were available to us students for consultation, which literally came to influence our thinking and our planning for our lives.

In my case, the influence began to operate in two fields: that of international relations, which was my formal major and reflected the interest that had grown up in my mind during the war in East Asia, and also the influence in the field of theology. In this area, it came under the influence particularly of the Rev. Professor Kenneth Latourette, who was not only on the faculty of Yale University but also the Yale Divinity School. He had a strong background in Chinese study and he had attended from Yale in his undergraduate years a tour in China at Yale's school 600 miles inland called Yalli Middle School. Under Dr. Latourette's influence, I not only attended some retreats in New York City and was exposed thus to the city in a way that would influence me greater in life, but I began to focus on the Yalli School in China as a possible assignment for me. I was then accepted for that assignment as a senior student and began preparing for it by taking Chinese lessons there at Yale.

Earlier in the winter of this senior year, I had experienced for the first time the feelings of falling truly in love. In this case, it was with a wonderful young lady who was a typical New Englander. A teacher at a not very distant girl's school, she was in charge of music as a qualified pianist and lived in the delightful little town of Bethel, Connecticut. There at the time of our acquaintance, she was living along with her mother who was a widow. I was fortunate to visit there from time to time and absorb the wonderful atmosphere of the small town. I undertook to take her to a concert one night at Yale University and then went with her on various outings, including one in the middle of a snowstorm. There, under my great guidance as a former

Southern Californian, we proceeded to get lost in the woods in the snow but fortunately did make it back to the house. I attempted to make it up to her by taking her for a ride on the coach's launch on the river. I was, of course, hoping that I would influence her with my great strength and expertise as an oarsman. As the light heavyweight boxing champion of the Ivy League, I was able to invite her to a boxing bout that I proceeded to win and then took her to the senior prom and appeared, of course, with a black eye that she very gracefully ignored. We attended a Yale football game together and she was able to spend the night in one of the Quonset huts occupied by my former roommate and his wife, as he had married by that time.

It became clear, however, that my relationship with this wonderful young lady should end with my assignment overseas, in China. I undertook to bring about that break in our relationship. I unfortunately did not do that in the frank way I should have done. Thus, I had acquired another lesson in life, imposed this time by myself. I have undertaken since then to avoid repeating that mistake. I did, however, have an opportunity by telephone, a number of years later, to beg her forgiveness. Clearly, through my relationship with her, I had gained a great deal in terms of acquaintance with New England life and surroundings and also success with my undergraduate education that would be the base for my subsequent five years of graduate work and a beginning of an all new second life.

This chapter is a story of two loves—the first is the enchantment by my new life in New England, which was to go on for eight years, ultimately, and the exposure to the new life as a student at Yale University.

The second love was my first experience with falling in love, and in this case with a beautiful young lady. We had a wonderful relationship during the best part of my senior year at Yale, in 1950. Our relationship ended at the time of my graduation. In retrospect, it seems to have been nearly set by the fate that took me into the fifty year career that I was to have in National Intelligence and the fifty-five-year marriage that was so much directly a part of that life.

This part of the story begins then with my arrival in New Haven, Connecticut, to attend YU, carrying with me the strong lessons that were laid out in past sentences from my naval experience and lessons that were to serve me throughout these years and on into the following years in a very important way.

As an undergraduate at Yale, my understanding and appreciation of NE (New England) was expanded through several experiences, but one particularly that remains forever strongly in my mind. My parents had visited from California and we had gone by auto to New Hampshire, specifically Franconia, New Hampshire, and there my mother was renewing contact with her agent, the one who was handling her manuscripts in child stories, and that visit took us to a delightful old inn in Franconia called Kinsmen Lodge. After that time there with my parents, I followed through as a student on vacation in the dead of winter at Yale. There was no thought of visiting my family back in California, partly because of the expense involved, but I was delighted to follow through on the contact made in Franconia, and I would literally take the night train from New Haven and arrive in Franconia very early in the morning and make my way to a farm that was perhaps five miles away from the train station. One time, probably the first time, when I started to walk that distance, the temperature was something like 40 degrees below zero. I was picked up by someone in a truck who told me I was crazy and gave me a lift to Kinsman Lodge. There I enjoyed the feeling of helping the farmer with pitching silage for the cows early in the morning before breakfast, and then having a wonderful breakfast made over a woodstove before heading out on foot through usually at least two feet of snow up to the woods for my day's work. My job for which I sought no pay was to take a long, heavy bucksaw and an ax and trudge about forty-five minutes through the evergreens to the hardwoods above. My purpose was to bring down enough trees and cut them up so that I could help supply the farmer his whole year's wood supply. After a full day's work, I enjoyed hearing the sound of sleigh bells coming up from the valley below, when the farmer would arrive with his horse and sleigh. We would pile up the five-foot logs that I had cut up during the day. We would both climb up on top and go careening down through the woods, ducking the branches on the way, and depositing the day's work at this farm. I would then enjoy a wonderful dinner at the lodge and sleep well before getting up at 4:00 a.m. the next morning for another day's work.

I took this experience three times as an undergraduate, and each time in Franconia, I enjoyed particularly remembering when I was there with my parents in the spring time. It was delightful walking along that road and soaking in the atmosphere of New England and occasionally talking to people and being surprised by their wonderful language and their type of speech, and hearing from the local people about the allure of Franconia, the presence of the home of Robert Frost, and the presence of the Notch, and the "Old Man of the Notch" as seen in one of the rugged hillsides there. I clearly came to regard these people as the salt of the earth and that stayed in my mind as I made other contacts in New England. I found people living out the aspects of New England life, which my father had described to me so many years earlier.

Another opportunity I had to develop my enchantment with New England in this case was farther down in the New York suburbs I came to my family's contact, specifically my mother, with a wonderful family in one of the major bedroom extensions of New York City. I would spend Thanksgiving or even Christmas with these wonderful people when I could not make it back to California. The wife was a well-known author who had published the Bobsie Twin series, and her husband was a former artist with one of the advertisement companies in New York. Catherine and Burton Keiler became known to me as Aunt Catherine and Uncle Burton, and they treated me as a son. It meant a great deal to me to have this additional exposure to a different way of life and people with very different backgrounds and experiences. At their home, for example, I experienced my first snowfall, having come as a freshman, probably, from Southern California. With them I also saw the beauty of Christmas decorations, there in the snow, and all the other aspects of that life that I had not had in Southern California. I couldn't count the number of lessons of life that I learned from the Keilers. Then ultimately, there was a direct benefit to me from them because it was through their daughter that I was introduced to the young lady who was to become the subject of the next part of this story.

I was first introduced to this wonderful lady with whom I was to have the first experience of true love. We were introduced at a badminton party, at which I proceeded to fall flat on my face. Not literally, but in this sense, I regarded myself as a fairly good tennis player, and not having played badminton before, I proceeded to use tennis strokes with great zeal, which is the last thing you want to do! It completely broke up the game and showed that I really didn't know what I was doing. In retrospect, the beautiful thing that occurred was this lady took me aside and explained the source of my difficulty and proceeded to pass it over as something perfectly natural and certainly nothing that was going to get in the way of a potentially good relationship. From that point on, that was what took place. In retrospect, it is somewhat surprising that the relationship did develop so well because she told me that she would be coming to the Yale campus one night each week to practice on the organ and that we could meet on those occasions. I took her up on it and after getting back from rowing and downing some food in a big hurry, I would make it over to the old campus area and I would wait, sometimes in the cold, hoping to see her. Week after week I would do this without success. Finally, we were in touch by telephone and explored this failure on my part, and she explained that I must have been standing and waiting at the wrong chapel, namely the Yale main chapel. All I would have needed to do was walk across the old campus to the other chapel where she was practicing. I came to know her as such a fine example of people in New England and their stature and their values. One day, I asked if I might visit her school and hear her play the piano at a performance that was scheduled. After some hesitation, she said she would welcome that but wondered if I would mind very much just slipping into the back row of the assembled people and not be identified with her on that particular occasion. I accepted on those grounds and she gave an outstanding performance. I understood that her concern was that the students would begin to focus on her having a contact, which would be a distraction for the students when she was teaching during the weekdays. I accepted that completely, particularly in light of the fact that she told me she was coming off a previous relationship with a friend that had failed and wanted to make every effort to avoid another failure. In retrospect, the tragedy is that that is exactly how it turned out and I take full responsibility for that.

Our relationship developed over many months in a very natural way, going to concerts at Yale, to the beach where we rented a rowboat, and I was in my usual way of showing off by demonstrating my great prowess at rowing. We also did a lot of walking and talking as well as sitting together in front of the open fire in her mother's home in Bethel, Connecticut. I enjoyed her piano playing and we did some singing together. We went ice skating on a lake, which was an experience I had never had before. I had skated on indoor rinks in California but was unprepared for the roughness of the ice on the lake and, needless to say, I did not skate as well as I had hoped.

On one occasion, my parents were in New Haven to see my graduation in 1950, and we went to the home of my friend, and my parents had the occasion to meet her mother. We went on from there to the beach for a chance to see New Haven Harbor, where my father had rowed very often amongst flowing ice on the water, which was in contrast with the rowing that I did on the Housatonic River. During that occasion at the beach, I found that my mother got along beautifully with this lady and my father was very standoffish, which was a surprise to me, except that I came to realize that he was concerned that I would become too seriously involved and he felt this was premature as an undergraduate.

My contact with this close friend ended with her taking me to the airport for my return to California to visit my family. Most regretfully, my return to New Haven to enter the Yale Graduate School went both unannounced and unexplained to her by me. All too many years later, however, I found the courage to telephone her with a very tearful request for her understanding and forgiveness, which she most gracefully provided.

Chapter Twelve

Multiple Acculturations

Finding My New Life through Others, Particularly Foreigners

My intensive Chinese language studies, which began after graduation from the class of 1950 at Yale, took me that summer into an exceptional opportunity to meet and get to learn from many foreigners at Yale. That, in turn, led to the wonderful marriage that was to carry me through graduate study and on into a full fifty year professional career in the Central Intelligence Agency.

This language study took place at the Yale University Chinese Language Institute, and I was there, extremely fortunately working under a nationally recognized specialist on the Chinese language. The lady Chinese language teacher had come from Peking and brought with her the teaching of a special teaching dialect of Standard Mandarin Chinese. Although told about the many different dialects in China, which I was told numbered well over a hundred, I was most happy to concentrate on Mandarin itself. In additional to learning the spoken language, the training involved the use of flashcards to bring about memorization of some 3,000 Chinese characters, which are essential for reading the so called "newspaper level Chinese."

In addition to this very intensive daily instruction, I had the privilege to be tutored by a nationally recognized expert on what was called analytical Chinese. In that court, I was blessed to become acquainted with the Chinese philosophical construct known as "Ai Chin," which was to become the theme for this very book.

As with all foreign language studies, face-to-face conversation is very important, and I was directed to the International House at Yale for an opportunity to get acquainted and converse with a very fine young Chinese gentleman who was studying in the graduate school. I, therefore, became a resident of the International House and was thus extremely benefited by the acquaintance of the twenty-four residents there representing thirteen different countries. All these outstanding people were studying hard in the graduate school in various subjects and were thus very important conversationalists for me in at least getting a feeling for their countries and their individual languages. The importance of acculturation, or the process of learning about another culture, thus entered into my thought process and my plans for the remainder of my own graduate study.

Fortuitously, that took me by the building that included the Registrar's Office. Lo and behold, I saw there another foreigner who had come to the United States from Germany and was recognizable as slightly different in some ways. She dressed more formally than others, she wore her hair in the pony style that was common then, but I detected a difference in her demeanor. In the Registrar's Office where she worked, she seemingly had been carefully hidden in part behind a large desk so that students would not necessarily come to meet her, but I managed to bring that about outside the Registrar's Office and was able to see that she went to lunch with the staff every day. The group of the registrar and his elderly staff, along with this newcomer, would walk in a line down to the middle of town and would always lunch in the same delightful old haunt called The Smoke Shop, which had a place for light lunches that this group always had, literally, every single day at exactly the same time.

Having stumbled onto this routine, it was not too difficult for me to find reasons to go into the Registrar's Office and carry out work of some kind that would allow me to view this young lady in the rear of the office. Having done so, it was a very welcomed surprise to find one evening at the International House, a chatting group outside on the patio that included this attractive newcomer. She was called Haya by all of the residents there, even though she had four formal names, specifically, Mary Elizabeth Doris Berne. I was therefore invited to address her as Haya. That led to our close acquaintanceship, and I was perhaps helpful in getting her a new job in the Student Appointment Bureau. This was a small, rather intimate, office run by a gentleman who found that this lady was an ideal one to work for him. She being absolutely bilingual, fluent in English and in German, had an approach that would make incoming students comfortable in pursuing their business questions. That experience in learning about all the students and where they came from and what their qualifications were placed her in direct line for an increase in position to the highest position available for a secretary at Yale, specifically, the secretary for the master of one of the residential colleges; in this case, Calhoun College.

Having received word that the opportunity to go to China for teaching there had been foreclosed by the involvement of China in the Korean War and refusal on the part of the Chinese government to provide safe conduct passes for Americans, my focus on Chinese language continued. I began also to focus more directly on the possibility of a major in international relations as a graduate student at Yale. This desire was increased in my conversations with Haya, which extended to evenings in the home occupied by the professor who had brought her to Yale University as an emigrant from Germany—he having been her direct supervisor in the occupation forces in Germany where he was serving as an officer in the intelligence services of the army.

Those often-long evening conversations opened up for me a whole picture of Germany failing in the war and then having to face the results in terms of change that would be required by the occupation forces. Specifically, Haya was serving in what was called at that time the DeNazification Division of the occupation forces, and because of her bilingual capabilities and other reasons, she had been given direct access to the central files in Berlin that contained the records of those Germans identified as Nazi leaders. As a result, over the period of the two years that she served in that position, she acquired a lot of very sensitive information. The time came for her to leave the country to be safe. This was arranged and the evening conversations covered the years leading up to that in terms of her experiences under Hitler and then under the wartime pact. The results after the war were very, very broadening for me.

I learned, for example, from her that her name, actually a nickname, Haya had been thought up by herself who called mother Maya and her father Paya. It became clear at one point that Haya, being an actual first name in Israeli circles, was potentially a danger for her in the Hitler regime and she was advised by close friends to drop it. In these evening conversations, she made it clear that she had chosen not to drop it, and even though her father had lost his very well-known publishing house because of his openly anti-Hitler stance, she took the position that she was going to maintain use of that name publicly, and she did so. I learned also about all of her early experience as a member of the Hitler period in which all young people had to work. She had worked as a servant for an itinerant pastor in Northern Germany in which circumstances were very difficult indeed. Conversations brought out detailed description of the bombing and loss of their family home and other specific instances in which her life had been threatened by the bombing. Another of the conversations addressed the experience of her father, Friedrich Vorwerk, who had to go underground for a period of roughly two years following the assassination attack on Hitler in which Hitler was not killed in the bombing. Therefore, Hitler pursued any of those who had any involvement whatsoever in planning for the attack.

My time with Haya was also spent during the day on weekends walking and talking and one night, for example, we went up on a nearby outcropping called East Rock and viewed New Haven below in the lights. On the way home, she asked if she could be carried by me. As a former oarsman for the Yale Crew, naturally, I wanted to demonstrate my ability to handle anything, so I carried her on my back for the better part of three miles to the International House.

My close relation was broadened to a considerable degree by the other residents in the International House. One was a Greek student who undertook to do his own cooking, as most of us did. He was using a pressure cooker filled with spinach one evening and the top blew off. This spread spinach all over the ceiling, and I, as the tallest one in the group, had the job of standing on a chair and wiping the whole ceiling. Other students from Chile, France, Britain, and Pakistan and other countries, including Scandinavia, added much to the broadening of my mind and thus preparing me for formal involvement in graduate studies in international relations.

At the end of that 1950 summer, I was prepared to marry Haya, and against the advice of my father, undertook to do exactly that. We went against his thought that I was still too young and too inexperienced to take on the responsibility of marriage. One of my strongest mentors, however, namely Reverend Professor Kenneth Scott Latourette, welcomed the idea and obviously thought this was something I was prepared for and would benefit from. He agreed to marry us, at our suggestion, in the beautiful tiny chapel at the base of the tall Bradford Tower on Yale's campus. All of the residents at the International House were highly supportive, and I was fortunate to be accepted as a special student in the graduate school in preparation of pursuing a master's degree, and after that, a doctorate.

Thus began for Haya and me a five-year life which we came to think of as our Golden Years because they started out living in the International House as a married couple, then for a year in the basement apartment of a brownstone house in town, and after that in the Veterans' Housing in one of the Quonset huts in the village.

Early on in that transition, Haya was heavily involved with the students at Calhoun College, and I, with my studies. We were very fortunate to have a summer break as residents at the home of the long-time secretary at the university whose mansion was on the edge of town. We, as a summertime resident couple, thoroughly enjoyed that contrast with the tiny Quonset hut. I was by this time working, in addition to my full-time studies, in various ways to earn money. The G.I. bill support had run out, and it was necessary to supplement the regular good income that Haya was getting as a secretary. I was able to do this in various ways, working in a factory, in a laundry, and as a door-to-door salesman for one period. Needless to say, our life was quite Spartan, and our biggest enjoyment was Saturday night walking the two miles into the center of town and buying the weekend New York Times that we would then pour over during the weekend.

Chapter Thirteen

<u>Learning the Value of Acculturation</u>

My acculturation for the German culture began with my wife describing her years as a youngster in the suburbs of Berlin, the capital of Germany, in a small community of intellectuals. Her father, Friedrich Vorwerk, was a distinguished publisher in the capital of Germany, so their home was a sort of Mecca for outstanding authors and musicians and others. His specialty as a publisher was coffee tabletop volumes of truly outstanding literature. At that time, he was beginning the publishing of some political tracks and that was mainly because of his anti-Hitler stand, which he very courageously took at that time. He was able to survive in that regard because of his reputation, but the Nazi regime soon took his business away from him and allowed him to live by some income from editing work for other publishers. Very early in my marriage to Haya, his daughter, I became quite acquainted with this very fine elderly gentleman, even though he did not speak English, and my German was very halting. His daughter, my wife, Haya, was a teenager at the time of the Olympics in 1936, and as a youngster at that age, she was involved, along with thousands of others, in a performance held in a stadium where Hitler was observing the Olympic Games. The youngsters were to carry out these athletic exercises, which consisted mainly of rolling large full hoops in which one would stand and turn upon one's self.

Haya's young life was further influenced by the Nazi regime in terms of the requirement that all young people at that age had to do some work. Her assignments were potato digging in various farms, and since she knew how to ride a horse, she came to be a driver of a wagon that carried the potatoes. This went on for some months, but after that, she had an assignment that continued for the rest of the period of her requirement. That was serving as a servant in the family of an itinerant pastor in the northern part of Germany. She would accompany the pastor in his weekly rounds and would be present to assist him as he gave his sermons. She described to me the wife of the pastor as being a very friendly lady but that he was not friendly, and this was not an easy assignment for her. She worked with him for a period of up to one year.

Haya was twenty years old when the bombing in Germany intensified as the United States entered the war. Her family began to feel it directly, which included severe damage to their home. She experienced bombing that affected her directly. One of her clearest remembrances was of running down the middle of her street toward her home with the houses burning on both sides. She recalled arriving at the already damaged house and finding glass not only all over her bed but she herself had a shard of glass that cut through her shoe into her foot.

As the war intensified and the impact in Berlin increased, the family arranged that she move to Vienna, Austria. She did that in a train, which was strafed by allied aircraft and she survived that alright. In Vienna, she became a secretary in the surgery department of a hospital that was receiving the German troops returning from the Russian front. She described often having to sleep there overnight. While the surgery continued, she took the notes given by the surgeons. She would have to sleep on a cot there without any real opportunity for rest. As the war ended and Austria was occupied by Soviet troops, Haya found that she was threatened in her own apartment house, but was very fortunately saved by a Catholic priest who arranged for her to be kept in a convent and labeled as a patient under serious care.

Upon her return to Germany, she found in Munich a job with the Allied Occupation Forces. Having been educated at an international school in Bavaria, Germany, she had a high degree of bilateral capability. This made her valuable in the Denazification Division, which was undertaken to separate former members of the Nazi regime into five sections. These would range from a designation for pursuing their people's former capabilities but having no ability to expand further in the economy. At the top of the range would be former Nazi officials who had engaged in war crimes who would be so designated and not be allowed to assume any position in the government of the German republic. Haya's contribution included her traveling to Berlin and engaging in retrieving from the central files the information needed in the Munich division of the Allied Denazification program. Over two years of such work, this activity brought her to the attention of those who were identified as threatening in some way and a decision was made by her supervisor, a major in the US Army, to assist her in emigrating from Germany to the United States.

Carrying that out in January 1950, she arrived at New Haven, Connecticut, at Yale University, and was sponsored there by this former major and his family. She lived near Yale University where the major was already on the faculty of Yale University in the German department. In the summer of 1950, when I was becoming well acquainted with Haya, I thus engaged with her in evening conversations with the Wood family and learned a great deal about the immediate wartime experience in Germany. Specifically, there was much to be learned about the way in which the German people reacted to the occupation and responded in terms of overcoming the feelings about the war and the need for a new start in Germany. There was much discussion about the way in which Haya's father had helped with the publication of a journal, specifically titled "Christ Und Welte." In English translation: "Christ and the World." It had a very significant role in helping the German people examine their own situations and consider avenues for the future in a truly democratic way, along the lines that the Republic of Germany had been known for in the early 20s, before the rise of Hitler to the leadership in Germany.

The major, under whose wing Haya had been brought to Yale University, had been a personal friend of Haya's father in the postwar period. These long evening conversations in which I was benefitted brought out much of the information about Germany's reaction during the war and the immediate postwar period.

In the following years, when Haya and I were married, her father visited us in the United States. On one occasion, I rode with him on the train to Philadelphia for an audience with the former director of the allied forces in Germany, who gave Herr Vorwerk a medal, recognizing both his contributions during the war and in the postwar period. I had been earlier struck by the request by her father to visit the grave of President Kennedy upon his arrival in the United States. His description to Haya and me was of the strong impact that President Kennedy had had upon the residents in Berlin in the postwar period.

My recollections of these long, edifying conversations with Haya and the family of her sponsors at Yale, and the visit by her father to our home in Fairfax City, Virginia, were greatly strengthened years later when I was involved directly in the job of declassifying documents on the Nazi war crimes under the Nazi War Crimes Act of Congress.

As I found in these long conversations and also in the contact with the other foreigners in the international house where Haya and I lived—a reflection of her wartime-born and developed sophistication—proved to be valuable for her in her contacts with the Chinese. In the summer of 1955, she and I went to Taiwan to work there in a university and her in a nearby school for American Foreign Service officers. My direct daily contact with a variety of Chinese became a very important experience for me. In observing Haya's acceptance by these Chinese, partly because of her sophistication and understanding of their background and needs for the future, I began to develop the same understanding and preparation for my own future. My direct contact was with a range of Chinese from young undergraduates, both those born and brought up in Taiwan, or those who had come over with family from the mainland of China after the Communist victory there over the Republic of China. The contact also included members of the university faculty, many of whom were senior educators in some of the outstanding educational institutions on the mainland who had escaped to Taiwan and who thus brought into their conversations with me their background and experiences all during the wartime and postwar period in China. I learned then from this spread of Chinese a fundamental characteristic that came to have a great influence on me in my work. It was a natural preparation on their part to accept me and my cultural background so long as I accepted them in theirs. I was teaching the young Chinese an exposure to international politics, which had been totally unknown to them. I was learning from them a reflection of what they had been through and what their families had been through in China during the war years. For me, this involved an acceptance of these fine Chinese as representatives of a people who had been through tremendous loss, as had been those in Germany, and those who had begun at least in Taiwan to think in terms of the future and alteration in their ways of life. In their cases, there was a need to examine and reexamine the rise of Communism in China and the decline or failure of republicanism in China under the Nationalist government and the need to look forward to either revival of that type of government in a democratic life or alteration in some way. I have learned from the studies at Yale, in the graduate school, that the Chinese were known as perhaps the most revolutionary people in the world, but at the same time, the least rebellious. I thus detected in these many Chinese, whom I had this very valuable exposure in Taiwan and, later, in my four years in Hong Kong, that these Chinese had an ingrown sophistication about circumstances and demands and opportunities. They had a hunger to learn in my course of teaching the prospects or different approaches to world affairs that would be facing them as Chinese people and the opportunities for meeting those demands in a variety of ways.

Returning some ten years later to Taiwan to serve there, I found the Chinese there had, indeed, begun to think about their future and the futures of their government in different ways, and that they were well prepared to accept information and influence from the outside. As very natural entrepreneurs, many of them were busy building their economic strength for the future, but at the very same time, they were beginning to think about the avenues into the future for the Chinese people, specifically, for China as a country of the future. I credited this to the natural sophistication amongst them that Haya and I had observed, which many of us observed from the Chinese who had escaped from mainland China. This was observable particularly during my four years of service in Hong Kong amongst those Chinese educators who had escaped from Communist China. During their years in Hong Kong, they were trying their best to prepare their minds and capabilities for the future of China. That obviously involved for them a certain acceptance of a fact of Communist success in China in contrast to the failure of the Nationalist Republican approach that had failed by 1949, and at the same time, these sophisticated Chinese in Hong Kong knew that their own futures relied upon their ability to adjust, to cooperate, and to work with those who were in control of China. In doing exactly that, they found for themselves a way back to the mainland of China and into the educational scene on the mainland from which they had been forced to leave. They found a new life and one that would be seemly valuable to the development of China in ways that we have observed from the outside.

My experience in learning of the sophistication of Germans who survived the failure of Germany and the Chinese who they had known and dealt with themselves before that, I learned a sophistication that was very valuable for me to accept in my thinking about the future that both those two countries have a capability for adjustment that is almost essential in these current times. It is an adjustability that those in the United States will certainly be required to exercise also.

Acculturation that I was fortunate enough to have over a period of some fifteen or twenty years, I came to appreciate very much the contribution toward that from the individuals with whom I worked. In the case of my late wife, Haya, there was a particular contribution that was perhaps invaluable in developing my own thoughts and plans for a career.

The pattern and length of my fifty year career with the Central Intelligence Agency is laid out in a separate book, entitled A Mercurial Intelligence Career—Between Two Book Ends, and was published by Infinity Company.

The point to be made here is that that book has been cleared by the Central Intelligence Agency and provides considerable detail about my years working directly with the Chinese in Taiwan and Hong Kong. It shows, I believe, the benefit that had come to me from the previous acculturation.

My basic interest in acculturation is traced back to my undergraduate years at Yale in the class of 1950. I focused my attention on foreign countries. The following graduate years were begun with the pursuit of a master's degree on the subject of foreign countries, specifically Southeast Asia, and namely, Indochina. In the following years, in the pursuit of a doctorate degree, the emphasis was on international relations also, but specifically, China, and then preparing myself to teach amongst Chinese. My teaching responsibility in Taiwan was that of not just introducing the subject of international politics for the students and also physical education in ways that they were not that familiar with, but also a particular way of thinking and acting that was totally new to the young Chinese. When heading the student labor program at the university, I was leading the students in menial labor that, hypothetically, amongst Chinese scholars, was totally unacceptable, and in this case, they were required to engage in it. As they began to do it and they were learning teamwork and learning something about themselves that they had not known before, they found that it was a very valuable experience for them. Years later, when I was back in Taiwan, the graduates from the years I had taught there told me flatly that they felt that experience was the most important one they had had in their undergraduate years because it had prepared them to work in consonant with foreigners, particularly Americans, with whom teamwork was essential. They found that their own self-confidence and esteem had been raised in ways that they had not anticipated before.

In retrospect, I found in my mind that much of this concern and interest on my part in acculturation, particularly amongst Chinese, was related not to just the acculturation through my wife with respect to Germany, but it was related directly in my mind to the subject of my doctoral dissertation. The subject was the issues of US and China relations between 1945 and 1949 before Congress, and the thrust of that dissertation was that China undergoing fundamental change was a challenge to the United States in terms of how it might best relate to China in a productive way for the future. The discussion in Congress was intensive but shallow. Many of the participants found that they were really lacking an understanding of how the Chinese were thinking and how they were reacting to the years of invasion and dominance by Japan. That superficial but very intensive discussion in Congress basically led to a standoff in terms of US relations with Communist China and also the Nationalist government, which then had arrived in Taiwan. The standoff was one of amenability on the part of the American representatives to grasp the situation in most fundamental terms and plan its relationship with those Chinese who could be the productive type for the future.

For me then, a lesson of all of that study on my part and the conclusions of the dissertation and the follow-up direct work with the Chinese on a variety of levels taught me the absolute value of learning about foreign culture in a fundamental way.

Our family's new life back in the United States began in the State of Virginia in 1962, specifically at Fairfax City. There we first occupied an apartment house and moved into a house that we had bought in one of the suburban development areas called "Mosby Woods." Our daughter, Ann, was in preschool and then kindergarten before we were headed back oversees. Haya had begun teaching German for the Central Intelligence Agency, and I had been serving in the office of National Estimates.

Again, therefore, we found ourselves headed for a fine experience in acculturation with the Chinese in Taiwan, this time in the capital city of Taipei. For officially CIA-cleared information about my intelligence career at this point and beyond, I refer to the previously noted book, A Mercurial Intelligence Career: Between Two Book Ends, published by the Infinity Company. My focus there is on our family in the overseas situation and again focusing on an amount of learning we acquired through our contacts there with the Chinese people. Ann was ready to start as a student in the American school in Taipei, and Haya would become very active in sports at the Grand Hotel facility and would become a well-identified woman in the shopping area and would bring back very helpful things that would improve our life there and after we got back to the United States again. My contacts with the Chinese ran all the way from the street level to the rather high levels of the Nationalist government in Taipei. In the course of all that, I learned a great deal more than I had already done amongst the Chinese university and the provincial capital of Tai Chung and over in Hong Kong with the mix there of Chinese from the Nationalist regime and the Communist regime.

Around us in the capital of Taipei were the beginning signs of change of focus away from a hoped for return to the mainland, and development of Taiwan as a new economic base for successful development. The prospects for tourism were beginning, and with the United States involvement in the Vietnam War as a factor, with military people from the United States coming to Taiwan for rest and recuperation, there was a distinct movement now toward the future. The pottery industry alone was a good example that was being encouraged by assistance from the United Nations by sending a specialist to Taiwan to encourage this and to provide instruction as requested. The port just east of the city of Taipei was not evolving particularly well, but the one at the southern end of the island, Kao Hsiung, was emerging as a potential leader in the area of container shipping. As a contrast, Taipei Chinese artwork was catching on, particularly with the exposure to tourism. The artists were freed now from the traditional ties they had on the mainland with their masters and their teachers, and their creativity emerged in a most interesting way. Some of them entered what became recognized and described by various ones as an Avant-garde in Chinese art and there were considerable sales of that type of production. Haya was amongst those who encouraged that development, and that encouragement also went with a number, those in what we came to call our extended family. It consisted of mostly those Foreign Service and other U.S. government officers serving in Taiwan who had previously served together in Hong Kong and then prior to that in Taiwan at The Embassy Language School. Since the children in those various families had grown up in the same period, that further bonded us all together, and as we then moved toward the United States and service in Washington, D.C., that contact continued very strongly.

The floating poker group that had started in 1955 in Taiwan was still continuing at this time, more than ten years later, and was to continue to and is still continuing at the time of this publication. It continues minus this member, however, because of my loss of complete eyesight. Well beyond the very low-stakes gambling, the group benefitted from exchange of experience in dealing with the Chinese in Taiwan, and Hong Kong, and the relationships held with those Chinese began to emerge in my mind as the lessons that I now lay out in this book.

The clearest cultural impression that remains in my mind from those many years of exposure to the Chinese is a comparability between the Chinese and the Germans, particularly with respect to their ability to have survived a loss of their country, in effect, to occupying forces and then an inability, at least in the case of the Chinese within

Taiwan, comparable to that of the Germans in getting back on their feet and dusting themselves off and looking into the future with a high degree of co-orientation and hard work. An important factor in this development of Chinese culture that I observed was a strong strain of nationalism, but a nationalism that was expressed with humility to foreigners. Humility, that which was balanced in their minds and in their expressions, to me certainly and to any of my colleagues, a pride about their long intellectual history. In my case, this included that which was made known to me with both pride and also discretion. A long standing experience amongst Chinese of what they described as mutually agreed bondage. Tracing it back many centuries to the foot-binding within the emperor's realm and all the way up to currently exercise practice at various places in Taiwan, for example, wherein there is both mutual agreement and sexual satisfaction amongst the parties involved.

The Chinese expression used in this connection is "Shwang Kung Pao." As with so many Chinese expressions, there is double entendre. In this case, the key words are both mutual and passive, as found in the first and second words. The same mix of words in the Chinese intellectual tradition is found in the phrase "Ai Chin," which is indeed the theme behind the title of this book. It can be translated as it is by Chinese in different ways, but the one I would offer here is familial love, the first word is love and second familial. The meaning, as reflected here in this book, is that of separate people coming together and responsibly and gradually forming a new personage. Obviously, we are describing my wife and me, but also, I want to stress here the addition of our daughter to that concept. Combining a German strain with an American strain and having her exposed heavily to Chinese influence, we believe she has formed a truly exceptional personage. She carries the strong industriousness of both the Germans and the Chinese and also the commitment to loyalty that is absolutely seen in the Chinese.

As a good student at the secondary level, Ann went on to have a fine, well-balanced record at her college in Lynchburg, Virginia. She has been working her way over the years through various types of employment; she has reached a very responsible level in a large company, Lockheed Martin. Throughout all those formative years and beyond, she displayed a truly Confucius type of family loyalty that would do credit to any Chinese. In the case of my late wife Haya and me, that loyalty and industriousness came forth in a most critical way during the final years of her life and the current years of my life, when moving from one level of medical support in our lives to another.

Fenton's parents

Fenton's family dog

Babcock family grouping for tennis
Fenton, Sister Dorothy, Brother Milton,
Father Thorpe,Cousin Henry Bray

Chapter Fourteen

Babcock Family Life Overseas

This story winds its way through Taiwan over to Hong Kong and back to Taiwan over a period of more than twelve years. It tells of the very wide exposure that the Babcocks had to a variety of Chinese, from the farmer to the leadership in the government of the Chinese Nationalist Republic. It begins with our departure from New Haven, Connecticut, after I passed my doctoral test.

With my notes for finishing my doctoral dissertation packed in my suitcase, we headed for Taiwan. We were honored to be traveling with the new representative of The Asia Foundation in Taiwan, who was on leave from Yale graduate school where he had been the lead guide for me in my international relations study. Professor David Nelson Rowe had an extensive background of exposure to Chinese, including good use of the language and a large collection of books on China and U.S. relations. He had a great deal of experience in East Asia that made him a very logical selection by The Asia Foundation to take the position as the representative in Taiwan.

Haya and I were very fortunate to be traveling with him because we would spend the first week of our exposure in Taiwan in his home in Taipei, the capital of Taiwan, and we were given an introduction to living closely with Chinese and how to develop one's relationship with them. Mrs. Rowe provided Haya with good advice about selecting servants and making arrangements for meals and movement in and about a new house that we would be occupying on the campus of Tung Hai University, where we were to live for the next three years.

Dr. Rowe was very helpful in making clear to us what we were observing there in Taipei, the Nationalists Republic government, which had been driven out of the mainland of China by the Communist forces and was getting a new life in Taiwan. Its arrival in 1947 had been rather stark because of the resistance by a very significant number of the resident Taiwanese, who had been under Japanese rule for fifty years and regarded the Nationalist intrusion as one they were not sure they could live with. In February of that year, in the southern part of Taiwan, a massacre occurred that became a turning point and, ultimately, a development of a way of living together between the Taiwanese and the mainlanders from China, which managed to get them through the years to come.

Dr. Rowe's introduction to Taipei for us thus involved evaluation of the militaristic atmosphere, the parading of soldiers on the streets and the banners that were very widely displayed, which called for "fighting back to the mainland" at some time in the near future. Loud, militaristic music was frequently sounded out over the streets from the loudspeakers. This was 1955, so the atmosphere of preparation for possible return to the mainland was still quite evident, but as you will find in this account, it faded rather steadily thereafter.

After our very helpful introductory week with the Rowe family, Haya and I took the train down to the provincial capital of Taichung, more than an hour away, to begin our life in preparation for living and working at Tung Hai University. Upon arrival, we learned that although our designated cottage on the campus was finished and empty and awaiting us, we would not be able to occupy it at that time because of a problem. We gradually learned that the reason was the refusal of the last farm family to depart the campus area. The farmer's land had been appropriated by the government and donated to the university. All the other farm families had left and taken the government's offer of different acreage nearby, and the financial agreement that had been reached with them. Although this farmer and his family of seventeen people lived in a one-room house, he had simply taken a position that he would not move. Negotiations with him were still underway. We had been assured that an agreement would be reached in due time.

Therefore, Haya and I moved into a small apartment in the provincial capital. Haya was able to get a job very quickly with the U.S. Embassy Language School nearby, which was teaching Chinese to officers in the Foreign Service and other government agencies. She took the position of secretary to the director. I took advantage of this delay to focus sharply on completion of the doctoral dissertation by doing all of the typing of it myself, at least in raw form, for mailing it to my aunt in California who would put it in the final required Yale form. We had a comfortable enough arrangement in that small apartment with only one real drawback. Next door to us was a building that housed a Chinese opera team, and they practiced much of the time at night. For those who have not heard Chinese opera, you need to be told that it is not soothing music. The other drawback was the potential for robbery. On the advice of various old timers in the area, it was desirable to have a dog, so we acquired a fine little Shepherd puppy that we named Heidi, who lived happily with us for three years there. While Heidi did keep us safe from the potential burglars, she did pose a real threat to me, as she tried to chew up my notes for my dissertation! Heidi later returned to the United States with us and became a local famous actress in the area just north of the Golden Gate Bridge in San Francisco, California.

We then finally moved up to the university campus on the nearby so-called mountain, it was actually called "Big Stomach Mountain." We discovered that our cottage was approximately eight feet from the house and yard of the reluctant famer and his family. That required a little mental adjustment on our part since the seventeen people living in that one-room house spent much of their time outside, particularly the youngsters, who went around most of time with very little, if anything, on. The chickens and ducks were always free to move around. There was nothing but dirt on the road and it was a very windy and rainy place. We learned quickly that this was a way of life across the road from us that was totally different from any we had been exposed to, but was a very important lesson for us. Although we had been assured that this family would be moving out very soon, it was upon our departure three years later that we realized that they were still right there next door to us. When we came back ten years later from living as residents in Taipei, we found that the farmer and his family were still there.

With a nice fence around our yard to contain our rapidly growing dog, Heidi, we were going to enjoy the location of our cottage, which looked down upon the whole beautiful valley below and across the valley through to the mountains behind. With the help of many members of the faculty who were old timers after decades of living amongst Chinese on the mainland and a few years already within Taiwan, we moved in very nicely and acquired our own furniture that we liked. We were able to make the most of our housing and turn our attention to the new life there very quickly. For Haya, this took the way of driving every day in a car that The Asia Foundation acquired for us. It was a very nice, small British car. She made a twenty minute drive down to the city for her work at the U.S. Embassy Language School and then came back at dinnertime. Dinner would be well prepared for us by the fine cook that we had acquired by that time. We had learned about him through an advertisement for the services of former Chinese soldiers who wanted to have work but who might not have trained as servants. That was true in the case of this fine young man, Chu, who was very readily taught Western-style cooking by Haya. He knew enough about the Chinese style and could make a good combination of the two for us. The services of a young Taiwanese girl as the so called "Amah" were arranged, who would handle all the house cleaning and laundry, as well as assisting the cook. Everything worked out quite well. We soon came to value this cook very highly for a variety of reasons. Even though he had only the use of one eye, he was very adept in the variety of tasks, and he was extremely loyal. His loyalty was demonstrated one day when we were gone. He was lighting his cigarettes with a lighter that spilled fluid on his hand and became badly burned, but he simply waited there for us to return. We thereafter became very loyal towards him.

For me, life there began with an introduction to the students. I was able to demonstrate my ability to communicate with them in their own language, which was, as far as I was concerned, Mandarin, as I did not know Taiwanese. Thanks to the fine teaching I had received at Yale, and the usage I had developed at the International House at Yale, I was able to win the acceptance of these young people. They understood that I would also be willing to speak English with them when they wanted to learn to speak English. There were about two hundred in this first class, about half men and half women in their late teens and early twenties. All of them were required to wear uniforms one day each week and engage in some training for a possible military service. On the whole, they were strongly dedicated to learn from the faculty.

I was very honored to be a member of that faculty. Another member was the head of the English Department. She had served in one of the finest universities in mainland China for decades and had been chased out by the Communists. She had put her heart into helping to develop this new university in Taiwan for the benefit of all Chinese. Nancy Cochran became a close friend of ours and was a very valuable source of advice on how to treat Chinese in a respectful way, such that we would win their respect in return.

Other members of the faculty were distinguished historians or other specialists who had been well recognized on the mainland of China and were now able to sustain, to some degree, their respect in Taiwan. They seemed to be interested in my presence because of my offering the students a course on international politics, which had never been offered in Taiwan. The course had to be cleared for presentation by the Nationalist government in the capital, and it was probably also attended by some of the students who were also reporting back to the central government on the approach that I took in this course. Two hours a week, I would lecture in English with translation by a young Chinese who was fluent in English. On Saturday morning, I would hold forth with a group speaking in Mandarin, which they seemed to welcome. It was essentially a seminar atmosphere where they could ask questions, most of which I could answer without too much difficulty, and it would get us into questions that were prominent at that time. Such topics as the future of the United Nations, and the question as to how the Chinese were to be represented in that new world body—represented by the Communist government or by the Nationalist government.

Although this course of mine in international politics had to be given special approval by the Nationalist government in Taipei, I was quite certain that one or two of the students were probably reporting back to the government in some way. I never had any negative feedback during the whole three-year period. I was told, however, that such a course was still barred in other universities in Taiwan by the government.

Throughout the three years of my assignment in Taiwan under The Asia Foundation, my major responsibility at this new private university was to plan, develop, and lead the physical education program. Although an athlete of considerable involvement at Yale University as an undergraduate, I had never studied physical education. So on the advice of Dr. Rowe, I used the library at the Yale athletic office, studying much of the summer, before leaving New Haven to help me in my planning of the program.

I found that my first teaching of physical education had to start in a very dusty little warehouse that was very small and had space for only one half of a basketball court. My focus, therefore, was on getting the whole athletic field made out of the sloping hillside on which the university stood. I turned to the local American Military Advisory Assistance Group for help. It put me in touch with the Chinese army, which was training bulldozer drivers at that time and welcomed the opportunity to send one or two up to our campus to help level off the hillside.

One day not too much later, we heard the bulldozers coming up the main road from the city and, at the same time, realized that there was a parade of farmers who had every intention of stopping them from undertaking the work with the bulldozers. As they pointed out, this had been their property and they did not want to have it changed. Their hope was to once again be able to use the land for farming, and if these changes were made, they would not be able to do that. Two of their leaders literally laid down on the road in front of the bulldozers and started writing their last will and testament on little brown sheets of paper, which is a Chinese tradition. I realized they were very serious and undertook to arrange for a meeting to discuss the question with the authorities at the university. We then met with the very distinguished president of the university who was a very old line scholar in the Chinese tradition. He was open-minded with this type of problem involving people, so we had an effective meeting. My suggestions seemed to be helpful, and it was arranged that the farmers would have the responsibility and be paid for the smoothing of the earth after the bulldozers had leveled it. They used ox carts and their own hoes and baskets, which were the traditional way of moving dirt for them.

Thus, the site formation took place over perhaps a whole week and the farmers arrived with the ox carts and began with their hoes and mattocks to move the dirt into a proper form for the athletic fields and the drainage we would need around the outside of the playing field. The farmers were duly surprised and seemingly quite pleased when they found me pitching right in with them with all of the means that they were used to using and I was not. I was able to learn, and worked shoulder to shoulder with them and this extended over two to three weeks of hard work out in the hot sun. Finally, a space for a very good baseball diamond and a standard running track below it in another level were completed, and also a level space for tennis and basketball courts, which the students hoped to have there. Finally, several weeks later, after a standard Chinese contractor had put the proper surface on the playing fields, things were ready for the students to enjoy.

At that point, I hired two assistants to run the program with me— one was a lady from the mainland, who would be in charge of all of the women's athletics, and also a young Taiwanese graduate from another university in Taipei, who was also fluent in Mandarin, as most of the Taiwanese were at that point. The program progressed well and I found that my use of only the Chinese language was welcomed by the students. It was also helpful in developing my language ability and my feeling of direct relationship with the rest of the faculty.

Throughout this period of many months of mostly outdoors work for me, Haya was very busy working down at the Embassy Language School developing new friendships for our family with the students at that institution. In our time off, we would have considerable enjoyment at mealtimes and engaging in indoor performances of reading plays. I recall taking parts in two plays, one play involved Marilyn Monroe. We duplicated that with a great deal of amusement, with my taking the role of the sheriff, after which I came to get that nickname amongst that group of friends. These wonderful American officials became lifetime friends of ours. After that, we served in Hong Kong, many of us, and again in Taiwan and back in Washington. We continued to learn a great deal together.

Back at our cottage on campus in the evenings, Haya did an effective job of running the household and guiding both of the servants and made close friendships with a number of the faculty people. Many of the students would come also from time to time just to exercise their spoken English with us in the evenings or on the weekends. That was mutually beneficial for us, too, as plenty of the Chinese language was involved.

As the physical education program took full form and was operating on a daily basis under the aid of my two Chinese assistants, I was free to take the place of a Chinese gentleman who had been for more than a year leading the program called the Student Work Program, which had been based on the example of Berea College in the United States.

In leading this Student Labor Program, as it was called, I chose to work directly and shoulder to shoulder with all of the students as much as I could. They seemed to appreciate this because this program was a great departure for all of them from Chinese tradition. Usually, students would not be involved in any labor, and this was, indeed, manual labor. The program did teach them teamwork and how to gain self-esteem by engaging in something new for them and carrying it out in the way that was expected of them. For me, there was great gratification in later years when I saw these graduated students and they told me that this program particularly had been perhaps the most important experience they had had at the university. According to them, it helped to prepare them for the contact with foreigners, particularly Americans, as they entered into the business world.

For me, the program was to bring a very interesting development in my own personal relationships. I had over perhaps most of the time already there, which was going on the third year, I had experienced a very distant and discretely appropriate acquaintance with one of the lady students. I could not explain it to myself, but there appeared to be a chemical reaction in my brain when I saw her in the classroom amongst the other students or in her laboratory. For example, I would see her working at her desk, while I was outside the window sweeping the walkway. I only knew for some reason that the young lady meant something special to me. This beautiful campus had very distinctive architecture. Thus, as I prepared to leave behind this wonderful introduction to Chinese culture, I undertook to take a little stroll with this one lady student. We went out into the field after dark and enjoyed the sights over the valley of the lights of Taichung, and we talked about the past nearly three years and her hopes for the future. In the course of that, she literally raised the phrase "Ai Chin." She raised it as an example of Chinese philosophical construct that caught my attention that evening because of the previous exposure to it when I was studying Chinese at Yale. She and I did not pursue the matter that evening for obvious reasons, but it stuck in my mind in a way that was then further advanced in the course of my next four years in Hong Kong.

This very special young lady and I parted in a way that would be expected of both of us and we did not see one another again for approximately six years. Upon visiting Tung Hai University after those six years, several of the former graduates were assembled to welcome me, and she was in the group. On that occasion, she and I stepped aside and engaged in a very warm embrace that was, of course, a big surprise for both of us, I believe, but it has stayed in my mind as a further endorsement of the meaning of the Ai Chin in terms of two people reaching out to one another after having established a firm base for doing that in a responsible way.

Before leaving Taichung, Haya was successful in finding a good position for our cook, Chu, at the Embassy Language School. There he was to be the office's all-around helper and we were extremely happy in later years to visit there and find that he had, indeed, found a new home for himself amongst the American officers. Many had come and gone by that time but new ones had come and learned that he was an artist. To our great surprise and happiness, he presented us with a beautiful Chinese scroll that he had painted, which was comparable to those that he was painting there and making available for distribution amongst the students. He told us that he, as a young man, had been brought up in Shan Tung Province, the northern part of China, on a farm, and had been trained as an artist by an itinerant artist. This was a well-established pattern in Chinese life in various parts of China. He had obviously carried that skill with him through all of the war years, and had managed to maintain it despite the loss of one eye. He was happily able to use this skill again in the surroundings of a good job at the Embassy Language School. We were ashamed that we had never realized this while he was working as a cook for us.

Upon leaving Taiwan, we profusely thanked the resident for The Asia Foundation with tremendous strength of feeling and also his fine assistant for the experience that they had made available to us over those three years. We then proceeded directly to The Asia Foundation Headquarters in San Francisco. There, I was to learn the job of being a program officer. Haya and I were happily located in a new home that we were renting on the other side of San Francisco Bay, beyond the northern end of the Golden Gate Bridge. It faced Richardson's Bay and we looked out at the Golden Gate Bridge through the beautiful, big bay window in our little house.

Commuting back and forth over that bridge every day, I returned in the evening with great anticipation to see my wonderful wife and the perfectly beautiful new baby daughter that she had with her. I will never forget the picture of our baby, Ann, lying in her playpen on the living room floor closely guarded by our shepherd, Heidi. That mental picture was matched only in my mind by that of arriving home and opening the door to hear my wife singing German lullabies to our beautiful daughter.

Some six months later, we were on our way again, but this time, with wonderful memories of the evenings watching the sun go down behind the Golden Gate Bridge and seeing the lights come on in the boathouses of Sausalito and with the lights of San Francisco hills rising in the background.

With the experience as a program officer in The Asia Foundation Headquarters under my belt, I was ready to go to Hong Kong as the assistant representative for The Asia Foundation there. For Ann, Haya, and me, it turned out to be a very developmental tour of four years. We had many exposures to Chinese culture that were brand new and very striking and balanced in our memories with the beauties of Hong Kong Harbor and the pleasantries of life there on the island itself.

Leaving the San Francisco area was not easy, for we had made many new friends, colleagues in The Asia Foundation, and others, and we also knew that we were going to be leaving behind our beautiful Heidi. We had concluded that the required six months quarantine in Hong Kong was just too severe for Heidi and we wanted her to have a happy new home in a safe neighborhood. Such was found in the friends who were our next-door neighbors and with whom we had become very close indeed. Upon our return, they would also prove to be quite critical in respect to our new lives after Hong Kong. At the time of our departure, we did not know it but we would be returning to find our shepherd already a star performer in summer stock productions. While we would return to our beautiful view out across Richardson's Bay, becoming residents of California was just not to be in the cards.

We had a very nice visit with my family in Pasadena, California, to say good-bye and to also have Ann baptized. As we left, I could tell that my father was still uneasy regarding our move. He still had not adjusted in his mind to my life as a government servant. I knew in the back of his mind, almost certainly, was the memory of the time around 1917 that his sawmill had burned down in Hoquiam, Washington, possibly as a result of arson by a German. He had to work closely with government representatives on the task of getting the mill built back as quickly as possible. Apparently, that was a very difficult time. The spruce lumber particularly produced by that mill was needed for the production of American military aircraft in World War I, but the efforts of the U.S. government representatives sent west to oversee the rebuilding of the mill somehow had rubbed my father the wrong way. My parents also lost their firstborn son, whose name was Thorpe Babcock, Jr., at about the same time as the loss of the mill. This diminished the hope that he carried in his mind that at least one, if not both, of his remaining sons would become businessmen. When I was an undergraduate at Yale, my father and mother had come to New York City, and during a visit there, I was introduced to a former classmate of my father's at Yale. He was an officer in one of the largest banks, and my father almost certainly was carrying the hope at that time that I, as a graduate of Yale, would move somehow into the business profession. This was not to be.

A warm family gathering at my parent's home in Pasadena followed the baptism of our beautiful, golden-haired daughter at All Saints Episcopal Church in the City of Pasadena. We soon departed again by plane to the exotic orient. I remember well on that long flight to Hong Kong, when I would be walking Ann up and down the isle, it was truly amazing at the amount of attention that she received from various other passengers. Four years later, upon our return to San Francisco aboard the SS President Roosevelt, we saw Ann, then at age four, receiving the same kind of attention from passengers, and we knew somehow that we were on our way toward developing an exceptional person. We sensed her being comfortable with both the English and Chinese languages, and that she was developing a broad horizon of perspective that would serve her well in the coming years of uncertainty and pressure.

Ann's first steps as a toddler were taken in Hong Kong as we settled into a very delightful apartment about a third of the way up Victoria Peak. Arriving in 1958, we took the rather hazardous flight that had been described to us by friends before our trip, where the plane literally flies between towering apartment houses on the new territory's side of Hong Kong Harbor. The plane landed safely at the Kai Tak Airport. Years later, it was outclassed by the beautiful and very large international airport at the distant end of the harbor. Upon our arrival, we sensed immediately at the airport the British influence in the police force—its training and use of the English language. We then went on across the harbor on the famous Star Ferry, before taking a taxi up to our new apartment. Settling in there required hiring servants, a cook, and an amah to take care of Ann. That was also taken care of through the assistance of the staff of The Asia Foundation office.

The view down from our apartment over the harbor of Hong Kong was truly overwhelming in its beauty. It also spoke about the importance of Hong Kong as a mixing bowl of humanity and a melting pot in the ways that we would soon experience. As a former helmsman on our ship during the war, my eye was caught instantly by the movement of large ocean liners and warships through the harbor, finding their way for anchorage at the far end of the harbor. Their presence scattered the many fishing junks and merchandise-transporting junks in all directions. Both Haya and I would stand transfixed on our veranda overlooking the harbor as this scene was played out before us. In the foreground beneath us would be the teaming streets so filled with humanity in an amount that we had not experienced before. Soon, as we were engulfed in this new world of people, we became very aware of the variety and mixture of languages, and so many different Chinese dialects. We learned, for example, the Shanghai Chinese speaking seemed to dominate in the circles of cooks in the community, while the Cantonese dialect dominated amongst the amahs serving the foreign families living in Hong Kong, although I was very fortunate in that the staff of The Asia Foundation office there had a fine group of people who could handle both Mandarin and their own Chinese dialect, plus English. I soon lined up a teacher who helped me to at least grasp the Cantonese dialect, which was dominant in Hong Kong.

For Ann, daily life focused around her walking trip over to the garden behind the big house of the British governor of Hong Kong. In that garden, she would be brought together with all the other amahs and their children for an hour or two of chatter and fresh air. Ann would then be brought back to our apartment and given lunch and put down for a nap, which went very well as a routine except for one occasion when a monkey literally swung into her open window. She, of course, woke up and the monkey had to be taken out of the apartment. Additionally, they prepared her for the very delightful evening when we would all sit out on the veranda and enjoy the view down over the harbor. Ann got along fine with the servants and they were a very good influence for her. Additionally, she was given the opportunity to spend time with the cook's grandson, and they became very good friends. During the course of a day, she would be exposed to three different Chinese dialects—the standard Mandarin dialect, the Shanghai dialect of the cook, and the Cantonese dialect of the amah, and English, of course. Her primary spoken language was Shanghai, which occasionally caused some difficulty at our house.

For Haya, the days filled up with visiting with other friends in the Foreign Service group and getting acquainted with shopkeepers in nearby neighborhoods. She especially enjoyed spending time at Cat Street, where there were endless opportunities to see fascinating items, including furniture for sale. Haya developed a fine eye for outstanding items. One that we particularly value was an antique sideboard made of rosewood. We learned later that it had been brought across the border from mainland China in pieces, carried out by escapees and then put together there in Hong Kong. It was truly an outstanding piece of furniture. With the required certificate of origin duly signed in hand, we left Hong Kong four years later, with that beautiful sideboard and low coffee tables. They have stayed with us all the subsequent years in the many homes we shared.

For me, the workday began with a trip toward The Asia Foundation office through the center of town and past the navy pier where there were always boatloads of sailors coming ashore, not too far from the Red Light District. That route then took me along a hillside that was covered with tar paper shacks that had been put up by the tens of thousands of refugees from Communist China. As there was no running water for these people, the daily routine for them was to walk down the long face of the hill to get their water for drinking and washing, and then to carry it all the way back up the hillside to their settling place of living.

The office of The Asia Foundation representative occupied a very nice location. I was introduced to the staff by the representative of The Asia Foundation. He was a wonderful man with considerable background and professionalism, who unfortunately had not long to live after that because of illness. The fine staff had been there for a few years and was very loyal to The Asia Foundation. It became clear that the staff knew that I would initially be responsible for breaking the "rice bowls" of quite a number of Hong Kong residents who had been serving under the former Committee for a Free Asia, the precursor to The Asia Foundation. In a typically Chinese tactful way, the staff members warned me that I would be visited by various Chinese who wanted to plead their cases for continuation of the subsidies, which they had received previously. Those stressed a negative approach towards Communist China in terms of warning the other countries of Southeast Asia about the designs of the Communist regime in China.

As our new and positive approach was going to emphasize a much different one to Communist China, the way I saw to deal with these fine people who had served loyally for several years was to offer them opportunities for supporting the new approach. That, in fact, was the way I proceeded. In the process, I was able to get through to some of them and win them over to the efforts that we planned for the future. They turned out to be extremely valuable in that regard.

After my handling the leadership in the office during the illness of the newly arrived representative, I was able to shift the focus of my effort to the field of education in Hong Kong. One key question was how The Asia Foundation could best help with newly arrived expertise from Communist China within Hong Kong and help prepare them for the day when they might be able to return to China and where they could contribute to a strong and viable China. This focus brought me into close contact with a number of senior British officers in the government and also leading educators at the University of Hong Kong. That experience led to relationships with friends that have existed over these many years and have been beneficial to my process of further developing my understanding of China. I was provided much encouragement from the representative of The Asia Foundation (TAF). He was a very senior academician from the United States, on leave for assignment with TAF. Such leadership also came directly from President Robert Blum, who was not only a very experienced professional but also strongly based in the academic field. He would visit Hong Kong from time to time and those conversations undoubtedly helped to focus the changes that we were undertaking there in Hong Kong.

The number of refugees from Communist China was growing rapidly, and within one month, for example, some 90,000 of them crossed over the border easily in the night. The British government turned back trucks of refugees to the edge of the new territories that fronted right on Communist China. The guards on the Communist China side had been ordered to turn their backs and let these people escape, the Hong Kong government would turn them around and send them back again the next day. TAF staff undertook to participate in the civic activity of assisting these mostly young people in these trucks to make it through the process of going back and forth by throwing into the trucks some day old bread that was purchased for that purpose.

Other participants in this civic effort were staff members of the so called "Refugee Colleges" in Hong Kong, many of which still had connections with the Board of Christian Colleges in China that had long supported and truly pioneered much of the educational advancement within China before the Communist took over.

Since my focus in this book is to bring forward the family life that I experienced overseas, I would refer readers of this book to the previously mentioned book, A Mercurial Intelligence Career, Chapters

Four and Five provide much more detail on my assignment in Hong Kong for those four years that I was there with my family. Chapter Five particularly explains how TAF became recognized by the Congress of the United States as a "National Treasure." In that process, it is obvious that Hong Kong played a distinct role. Here, therefore, I will confine myself to emphasis on one project particularly, that of the formation and development of The Mencius Foundation.

As a successor to Confucius, who is quite well known internationally, Mencius was perhaps less well known outside of China but should be particularly recognized for his contribution to Chinese philosophy of the concept of democracy. Although quite limited throughout Chinese history, that concept has survived even under the Communist regime in China. It persists within clear limitations and the Chinese well recognize that it is traceable back to Mencius as the predominant philosopher of that period. Democracy suffered the experience of the Nationalist Republic of China, which was taken over by the Communist regime, but that democratic approach followed the Nationalist Government to Taiwan. It was in these years flourishing there in a way that may possibly be of some exemplary value for the Communist to observe.

For The Asia Foundation, it was logical enough to support the foundation and development of The Mencius Foundation in Hong Kong as a springboard for assisting refugees who had come from educational institutions on the mainland of China and who had hopes for returning someday in the future. In its meetings and discussions and its support of publication, The Mencius Foundation made a distinct contribution to the educational and political base in Hong Kong. Much effort then proceeded to refocus its attention towards Communist China and open the way toward the establishment of the New China University, which became the leader for Communist China in focusing its attention on sound economic development involving beneficial contact with American corporations particularly.

The Mencius Foundation owes its success and well-known reputation in Hong Kong to the leadership of Dr. Francis Pan who, near the turn of the century, was the first Chinese to have earned a doctoral degree in the United States. Dr. Pan and his wife Cecilia stood out in Hong Kong circles as leaders of preparing for the future and the refocusing of attention back toward Communist China. This direction was not hindered in any way by the fact that the brother of Dr. Pan was the current librarian for Mao Tse-tung, the leader of Communist China. For me, obviously, the relationship that I was able to develop with Dr. Pan was a great opportunity. I was fortunate enough to have the chance to develop it with him in a societal way and learned a great deal from him and his wife about Chinese culture. The Chinese philosophical construct of Ai Chin, which is the theme of this book, is indeed traceable back to the influence by Francis Pan and his wife on me, my tour in Taiwan, and my training in the Chinese language at Yale University.

My luncheon conversations with Francis Pan were focused on The Mencius Foundation and its plans and prospects. The evening sessions that Haya and I had with Francis and Cecilia were on the subjects of Chinese history, politics, culture, and people. In a display cabinet in their apartment overlooking Hong Kong Harbor, for example, they had a pair of the tiny slippers that were identified as originating in China. They offered an explanation that is perhaps unknown to many other people. It related far less to the confinement of the lives of concubines from early years on but pointed in the direction of the possible satisfaction of constriction in later day and life. We knew that the subject of bondage was one that would not be discussed by the Chinese except in much known circumstances, but in this case, Francis and Cecilia spoke about it relatively freely and addressed other aspects of Chinese life and culture that were very eye-opening for us.

In the recounting of their own lifetime experiences during the war and during education in the United States, they literally addressed the question of Ai Chin as a philosophy having meaning for special people. In effect, they directly or indirectly presented themselves to us as examples of an Ai Chin couple. They had somewhat parallel lines in the course of their lives because they possessed a strong base, felt free to lean toward one another, and discover through frank conversation those aspects of life that they shared and then were able to draw together in marriage. Thus, they created a new identity. In retrospect after all these years, I certainly carry them as such a couple in my mind, and I believe that was true in the case of my late wife. There is no doubt in my mind that Francis Pan and I had something in common as respect to our focus on international relations, and I think that is why we were drawn together as two professionals in a set of circumstances that provided considerable positive demand on us intellectually and in terms of action also. We certainly shared the same impression of why the Nationalist government had failed in its control of the mainland. We also shared our expectation that the Communist government would encounter very serious difficulties in extending its control thoroughly throughout Mainland China at least in the future.

Although my work in downtown Hong Kong and in the new territories across the harbor was very engrossing and demanding from time to time, on the weekends, I made every effort to break away for a chance to spend more time with Haya and our growing baby daughter. This was enhanced particularly when we moved to the other side of Hong Kong. There we had a very fine facility overlooking the beautiful Deep Water Bay, complete with servant quarters and parking space below. It was there that we found a wonderful life for the three of us. Haya and Ann spent most mornings right at the waterfront, which was just a walk across the street. In the afternoon, they would spend time napping or preparing for the evening events, which too often involved partying with good friends. We were very fortunate indeed to have wonderful colleagues with whom we had gotten acquainted with in Taiwan when they were in the language school. They were in a pattern for the most part of hosting one another for dinner and dancing afterwards at their apartments. We were also very fortunate to be invited by those who had so called "pleasure junks" to accompany them for picnicking on the surrounding islands, which were perhaps half an hour sail away from Hong Kong.

On one occasion, a group of six or seven of us reestablished a poker club, which had met for several years in Taiwan. It continued in Hong Kong and then for decades because the participants would be sent to the same country by chance and would continue the tradition. On this occasion, the group took one of the pleasure junks and went overnight. After playing poker, we slept on board in a cove not too far from Hong Kong Island as we thought that this was a quiet, private place to be spending the night. To our great surprise, we awoke in the morning completely surrounded and pinned in by fishing junks filled with families, babies, children, and fishermen, and we obviously were totally unaware that they had arrived in the middle of the night.

On the weekend daylight trips to nearby islands, the children particularly enjoyed picnicking. They were growing up together at approximately the same age, were becoming very good swimmers, and, on the whole, were getting a fine experience there that made them very healthy and happy. For me, weekends with Ann was a great opportunity to enjoy her company and observe her growth. We would get up early and walk behind the building where we were living into the hills and come to places that had been active waterfalls and now there was no water. It was frequent that the place would be totally dry. Ann was of a nature to climb them and she became quite a climber later in her life, partly traceable back, in my mind at least, to those days when she could do that safely within my reach while growing up. On those occasions, we would also often stop by a farm that had a pony that would be available for children to ride and she also possibly traces back her desire to have riding lessons in the United States to that very experience in Hong Kong. My clearest memory of her in those years in that apartment overlooking Deep Water Bay was when I would find her in the kitchen seated beside a little boy who was the grandson of the cook. Both of them would be chatting a mile a minute in Shanghai dialect Chinese and practicing their calligraphy at the table. She truly developed a good, firm base for pursuing that language and that served her well in our next assignment, which was in Taiwan. There in the American School, the study of Chinese was required. It was there that her exposure to Mandarin would become even stronger.

One of the places that we did not drive to visit as a family was the abandoned school out on the east end of the island. It had been used during World War II by the Japanese who had taken over Hong Kong to put the residents in Hong Kong in confinement. A very large number were confined in that place for several years before the end of the war released them. One of the memories some of them passed on to us was that the Japanese chose to use the beach beside that building as a place to execute those who they wanted to behead, and that kind of memory for some of the people was very difficult indeed.

For me, perhaps one of the strongest memories of Hong Kong was the annual meeting of The Asia Foundation representatives who had come in from all fourteen of the countries where they ran The Asia Foundation offices. At those conferences, they would report to the president, Robert Blum, the work that they had accomplished during the past year. I was very fortunate and honored to be the reporter for those meetings and, as a result, learned a great deal that I might otherwise not have known. I was very fortunate in broadening and deepening my own perspective at that point.

When the time finally came to leave Hong Kong at the end of our four-year tour, we were fortunate to travel on the newly renovated luxury cruise ship, the SS President Roosevelt. Prior to the remodel, that ship was a transport ship during WWII and, in many ways, was given a new life with its remodeling. We had a very nice farewell from so many wonderful friends we had developed over the years. On board the ship, we found that our four-year-old daughter had attracted the attention of a number of the passengers, including the president of the line, who liked to swim with Ann in the swimming pool. It was wonderful for her to have that attention by various people. One time, some passengers came out onto the deck to seek out Haya and me to come and watch our daughter in the ballroom who was with others using a hula hoop. One night, when a movie was going on, walked into the viewing room in her nightgown, having left the side of the steward who had been accompanying her from our cabin, which was nearby.

Our arrival in San Francisco under the Golden Gate Bridge was a very warm occasion. We knew that we were returning to the lovely little house that we had previously rented in Marin County, north of San Francisco, with that wonderful view of the Bay with the Golden Gate Bridge in the background. Upon arrival at our home, we were presented by the neighbors with a very large sheaf of newspaper clippings about the performance of our previous dog, Heidi, as the star of a summer stock plays about Rip van Winkle. The next morning, we were delighted to see her in the company of the paperboy and found her very happily connected to him. She did remember us very warmly and that made us feel very much at home again.

It was a short time, however, before we were visited by the former Yale history professor who had become the head of the national Office of Estimates at CIA's headquarters in Langley, Virginia. He invited me to go there to resume my career. That, of course, meant saying good-bye to many new friends in The Asia Foundation. It was only a short time before I was learning about the fine work the Central Intelligence Agency had been doing in the interim.

Fenton at Sun Moon Lake in Taiwan

Milton and Fenton at Long Beach, CA

Daughter Ann with Ling in Hong Kong

Chapter Fifteen

Further Professional Development

Benefitting as before from strong leadership and good mentor influence, I was assigned, upon return to Washington, to the Special Research Staff of the Deputy Director for Intelligence. It was logical for me to pursue the waning zeal of some of the leadership in Taiwan to fight back for the "mainland." By this time, the United States had a treaty calling for defense of Taiwan from a possible military attack by Communist China. It was important to see if the Nationalist Chinese hoped to "start a prairie fire" on the mainland was truly an empty hope. My conclusions on this subject after considerable research were well received and led to my representing the CIA on a group designed to further access and contact with the academic community in the United States on the subject of China's future. This, too, led to my direct involvement in promoting a new organization that would assist agencies in the United States in meeting the problem of understanding and translating China's language development, particularly along technical lines, which had been unavailable and screened off from the American access and understanding for many years.

This promotional effort on the part of the CIA led me into direct contact with a fine leader of the new Chinese English Translation Assistance (CETA) group that pioneered the effort that proceeded over the years to address not just the Chinese language but also the so called exotic languages. The driving force in this regard became the Multiple Language Management (MLM) group that was founded and led by Jim Mathias. My relationship with Jim was to continue over many years and be productive in various ways.

Another stimulating experience came my way while with the Special Research Staff. It was participation in a seventeen-week course designed to introduce one to the rapidly developing opportunity of computer use. That schooling was hard for me because of my nontechnical background, but it certainly opened my eyes to the demands of the future and prepared me in part for my next assignment as chief of the China branch of the Domestic Collection Division, then known as DCD, of the Central Intelligence Agency. It was well recognized and publically identified in the major cities of the United States as the avenue for volunteering information on foreign affairs to be evaluated by the CIA and then distributed throughout the intelligence community in Washington for the benefit of the agencies concerned.

Over many years, this avenue was used by loyal, private American citizens to pass on information on foreign affairs that they recognized as potentially valuable for distribution for the benefit of the U.S. government.

Our China branch was particularly concerned with preparing for the possibility of Communist China opening up for access by other countries, particularly the United States, and the possibility, through the Domestic Collection Division (DCD), of gaining valuable information.

By 1973, it was logical for me to accept an assignment to DCD's long-established office in New York City. The effectiveness of this assignment was clear to me on two counts, but it was to be discussed very carefully with my family because of our daughter's education and the new home we had just purchased in Vienna, Virginia. Professionally, the move for me would be a logical one because of the new experience in New York and the additional responsibility there. In addition to that, New York City was an attraction to me because of what I heard all my life about Manhattan from my mother. She had been brought up there by an aunt in an apartment on Central Park South. She had rolled her hoop in Central Park and studied piano at Carnegie Hall, and had accompanied her aunt while she, as a licensed artist, was copying in the Metropolitan Museum. In this career question, however, it was vital to weigh the fact that Ann was in a high school nearby our home. Another factor was that she and Haya would be living alone there except on weekends, when I would plan to return from New York by Greyhound bus and be with them at least for two days each weekend.

Our home was a lovely, old, turn-of-the-century farmhouse on one and a half acres with two barns and a chicken coop that we had turned into a greenhouse and potting shed outside. Upon entering the house, one passed into what Haya called the "diele," a low-ceilinged entry room with an open fireplace and beautiful handmade brick flooring. That rather unique flooring passed throughout the fairly large kitchen, which looked out to a grove of beautiful holly trees and other evergreens. Looking the other direction through the house, one came upon a magnificent Blue Spruce tree that dominated the bay window looking out on to the backyard and the barns. Upstairs, Ann had her own spacious bedroom looking out onto the top of the downstairs roof. The master bedroom was separated from Ann's room only by one bathroom, and therefore, the thought of my being away during the weekdays was, in my mind, a manageable one particularly because our beautiful large Collie dogs provided some additional security.

Ann's school, Oakton High School, about one mile, was walking distance from the home, and she brought to our house many of her friends who were also in the Explorer Scout group for evening discussion on the outdoors and other subjects of their interest. The downstairs living quarters were to remain unused during my absence in New York City.

With the approval of the family, I was off for a two-year assignment in New York and found lodging quarters there some walking distance from the office. I enjoyed the quarters of a former opera singer who was on tour in Europe for approximately one year. Upon his return, I then was able to benefit from a lead by a Chinese gentleman who was a well-recognized maker of violin bows in Manhattan and was a personal friend of a concert violinist, named David Sackson. Through this introduction, I undertook to occupy every evening after work his studio. It was for his benefit as well, as I provided security for his collection of many valuable violins. For me, it was the availability of a nice, small but certainly well-located and fairly quiet place for living at 78th Street, only one block from where my mother had been brought up.

When launching into this life of demanding work in the unique world of downtown Manhattan, I realized that I was following in the track already set by my wife, Evelyn, who had been there two years earlier. She was selected to go to Columbia University in preparation for launching a kindergarten program for the Fairfax County school system. Evelyn, too, had become a strap-hanger during many of her days and was thoroughly engrossed in the study that was required of her except on weekends, when she also took the Greyhound bus going back for the weekend to be with her husband in Falls Church, Virginia.

After a full day's work, my weekday evenings in New York City came to be committed to a mission of the St. James Episcopal Church, the church I attended at 71st and Madison Avenue. It was a mission that I was attracted to particularly because of the circumstances of my own parents. My mother and father were then still living in Pasadena, California, where I had been brought up. Both were in their mid-nineties, and the question of their futures became the subject of family discussion. In my case, I saw some mutual benefits in the course offered by my church on Death and Dying. I thus enrolled in a one-week course and found it very satisfying in many ways. Under the program guidance, I was to spend productive time with terminal case patients who were wards of the City of New York. So after making dinner in my small kitchenette, I would walk to the various hospitals or nursing homes and develop a relationship with a particular man or woman who had been designated as one who might welcome that kind of contact. Needless to say, it was challenging to make sure as much as possible that the time was truly beneficial to the patient. In retrospect, I believe that I, as a result of the training and experience I gradually acquired, was able to add perhaps substantially to the final days of these fine people. I certainly learned a great deal about the outlook of people who were facing the end of their lives.

In my memory, one case stands out particularly as one that taught me something. This was an impressive lady who had been brought up on a farm in New Jersey, had become a resident of New York City, and who could not assure me that there was a member of her family still available in New York City. She, therefore, upon dying, was given a short but quite beautiful ceremony at our church. I attended to carry out a commitment that I had made to her before she died. Upon attending that simple ceremony, I found myself looking back toward the rear of the church and saw a single middle-aged man watching but not taking any steps towards participation in the ceremony. I got the impression that he knew the purpose of the ceremony and that he had made some effort to be there. It had not been widely advertised in any way, and although I did not take any steps to meet him, I left with the impression that, somehow, the family relationship had been fulfilled.

Since my weekends were spent at home in Vienna, Virginia, I did not have that much time for socializing in New York City, but three people particularly stand out in my memory as those who influenced me greatly about New York City life. First, I would mention the outstanding elderly lady who was spoken of by other members of the congregation as the "church mouse." It did not take me long to find out how important she was at the church at keeping her hand and her eye on so many different things, and doing it so proficiently and so gracefully. We became acquainted over lunch a few times, and at one point, she invited me out to her apartment to see how she lived in the suburbs of Queens. My conversations with her brought out the fact that she had, indeed, been directly involved in intelligence during World War II as a staff member of the British station in New York City. She gave me a book that described the great contribution made by the British during the World War period. This wonderful lady basically taught me how to think about New York City on a daily basis, and I was fortunate enough to introduce both Haya and Ann to her during their very brief visits to New York City. They both felt along with me the warmth and commitment of such a person to the task of helping someone else understand and accept the way of life experienced in Manhattan.

The second friend whom I came to value highly was a member of the congregation, a lady who poured the tea for the regular gathering of the members of the congregation after service. She and I initially met as fellow attendees in the death and dying program at the church. It was with her influence that I became serious about the program, which I benefited from not only personally, but as I learned later from my parents, they too had benefited.

She occupied an apartment on Park Avenue and had long experienced that life, during which time, she raised children. She brought out the fact that she, at an earlier age, had somehow hoped to enter the intelligence service but that had never taken place. What this fine friend demonstrated to me was the caliber of people who moved in her circles and who undoubtedly were the bedrock for institutions in New York City, which contributed greatly to the lives of the wide variety of people who lived in that very busy and demanding city. The third person, who had such a strong effect on me during those two years in New York City, was a concert violinist, David Sackson, who with his wife ultimately became close friends of mine and Haya. David was truly a professional musician who lived in a world of his own, and one I would say, to some degree, a very important aspect of New York's life. He and his wife, who was then heavily involved in the music field, were in a managerial relationship. They showed me the treasures of the life of living in New York City, and how to benefit from all of the musical and other performing arts there.

After returning to our family life in Vienna on a regular, full-time basis, I turned to the question of my parents' need for assistance in the ending stages of their lives. It began with a family gathering called by my father at their home in Pasadena, California, which was attended by my sister, brother, and me. I, unfortunately, was rather rushed by my travel coming all the way from the east coast. My sister came from the Pacific Northwest. My father opened with the statement that they were planning to sell the house on LaLoma Road, Pasadena, and they were open to comment on where they might find a new place to live.

Since my family and I had very recently acquired the rather spacious property in Vienna, Virginia, my suggestion was that they move into our newly acquired house. When they got the nod for proceeding, I, upon return there, undertook to improve, rather extensively, the whole wing of our house that would be made available to them.

The reworking began and continued steadily for several months, for a total expense of $4,000 to be divided with my parents. I was only somewhat apprehensive about the plan because of commentary by very close friends of my parents, whom I also knew quite well. Upon seeing them for dinner prior to my departure from Pasadena, they were strongly against the move and made their commentary on their own circumstances, which involved a near-disastrous situation where they, as parents, intruded.

Some months later, when my parents arrived at our home, the plan got off to a bad start with a four-day delay waiting for the drying of the very intensive painting that I had accomplished in their part of the house, because of the very steady rain in the vicinity. Upon their arrival at the house, my father took me aside and surprised me by saying, "Son, you and I have both made a fundamental mistake, and we must get ourselves, get the whole family, out of this in the best way that we can." The subsequent weeks, and extension into months, did become very tense, and unhappy for my wife, daughter, and, ultimately, for myself when I began to see the evidence of relationships being very stressed.

One indication was the quite frequent telephoning of my wife to Germany to talk with her sister in the German language in commentary on the situation, in which I could understand the very negative approach. The relationship between my father and my wife became particularly tense, and showed in his case a basic dislike for Germans, which seemed traceable back to his circumstances during the First World War, when his lumber mill was burned down and he thought it had been done by German agents.

Finally, the time came for all of their household furniture to be returned to California where they now had purchased a house on the beach near Monterey, California, where they had always enjoyed the summers. Their automobile, which had been driven all the way for the stay, had to be returned to California, and a payment for the fixing up of the whole wing of the house that they occupied had to be arranged between our two families.

Needless to say, the departure of my parents at the airport to return to California was very tense and certainly unhappy on both sides. It was clear to me and to my wife that our daughter Ann had borne the tension in the house for those six months. In fact, we were thus glad to have that situation corrected. Then when I received the information that my mother was ill with cancer, it was further clear that the original decision for their moving to the east coast had been a fundamental mistake.

I visited their new place in the Monterey area and continued to keep tract of their health developments, and in the case of my father, I was there only a few days before the end of his life. I was comforted by the fact that as he and I spoke very intimately, he responded so positively to the conversation I had with him about preparation for dying, which he welcomed greatly. The benefit was that he was able to discuss the situation; as he put it, he had never been prepared as a product of New England in which that subject matter, in his view, was not normally discussed. He made the statement that, "You, Son, have just given me the best gift of my life by talking with me openly about the prospect of my death." That was clearly a step for him to make such a statement and indicated to me that the experience I had in New York City had paid off. Perhaps that so called gift to him helped to balance off some of the tension and unhappiness over the plan for the moving in with our family in our home in Vienna.

Some six months later, when I was out in Pacific Grove at their beautiful little, which they bought upon returning from Vienna, Virginia, I was able to spend some truly treasured time with my mother on the eve of her death. I think it possibly was also helpful to her that I had had the experience in New York and that I was able to speak frankly with her. She had had no reservations about discussing the subject. The result was that she advised me very directly that I should depart without waiting for her imminent death because I was to have surgery at the National Institutes of Health that could not be postponed. So I did, in fact, depart. As she had round-the-clock care by the two trained nurses, I felt that she was well cared for. My sister and brother-in-law also understood that I had done my part to care for my wonderful mother when they arrived at the time of her death.

These memories reflect the extensive thought and effort on my part to support my parents' final years and also similarly echoed in Evelyn's life as well. In her case, such thought and effort on her part were extended over a considerable period of time and commitment, and were directed at her immediate family and beyond. In both our cases, these events affected us as we proceeded along parallel lines in our lives.

WWII Attack Transport APA 202 USS Menifee

Haya with Fenton receiving masters degree

Fenton with family members

Chapter Sixteen

<u>Shared Lifetime Achievement</u>

As before, I benefited greatly from the fine mentoring and collegial assistance in the three directorates at the CIA at which I served. Continuing to follow the mercurial pathway already laid out for me, I served in ways that are described in the detail cleared by the CIA's Publications Review Board in the already published book with the title A Mercurial Intelligence Career: Between Two Book Ends. Leading a team in evaluating human source intelligence, I then turned to planning of covert actions overseas. This was followed by my participation in the preparation of the new Counterterrorist Center, before moving to the assignment in the Intelligence Community Staff. This included work on the tasking of collection and evaluating of human source intelligence.

Having already passed through the CIA's Mid-Career Course and also the Senior Officer Development Course, my status changed to that of a contract officer when serving for the remaining ten years of my career on the declassification team.

Those were long and engrossing years working with a fine group of experienced officers on the response to the Kennedy Assassination Act of Congress, the Nazi War Crimes Act of Congress, and the State Department History of the Bay of Pigs Invasion of Cuba. My active service ended with writing a formal operational history of The Asia Foundation just before I lost my sight. The work of the previous thirty-some years benefited greatly, as in the previous years overseas, from the strong support provided by my wife, Haya. During the latter part of that period, the CIA's strong educational loan program helped us put our daughter Ann through college, which prepared her for her future life. During these years, my family's attention had logically turned to preparation for the years after my retirement, with the result that our large house in Vienna was sold and an apartment was bought in Oakton, Virginia, where Haya was able to enjoy the swimming pool after her volunteer service at the nearby Fair Oaks Hospital.

Much weekend time during those ten years was spent in building our house on the Blue Ridge overlooking Shenandoah Valley. Some of the accompanying poetry was written there at that lovely house, nesting in the five and a half acres of heavily wooded land and was regularly crossed by deer making their way down to the Shenandoah River below. The great amount of labor involved in developing this property included our family members and many friends. For me, it represented a helpful balance with the rather demanding work at the office.

In developing this property on the Blue Ridge, it became apparent that this was an unusual piece of property. The long driveway had six switchbacks created when it had served as an old logging road in the years before. Many weekends were spent clearing the land at the top of the driveway and preparing it for the actual erection of a house that we had undertaken to build. The plans involved eight-foot long sections of the modular house, which we had brought in by truck, and placed in the basic position for the house. We had to do all the preparations in terms of the foundation, the exterior finishing, and interior of the house including all of the plumbing and wiring.

These long preparations extended over many months and, as mentioned previously, were accomplished with the assistance of family members and good friends, some of whom were qualified carpenters. The house took form and we truly fell in love with its deck extending around two sides and looking down over the valley toward the river. Most of the logging that was done to prepare the site and provide a reasonable view down into the valley was done by me with the assistance of a neighbor who had a Clydesdale horse. By sharing the logs with him, the job was manageable and served as a fine physical outlet for me from all of the concentration on the job at the CIA.

The accompanying original poetry was done by me and attempts to convey some of the beauty of this wonderful retreat. It also shows the sense of satisfaction obtained from the direct exposure to nature in its many, many forms, such as the beauty of the woods and the wildflowers, and the presence of animals in the daylight and at night. Naturally, we were going through all four seasons of the year several times in the process of getting the house available for living. We had a woodstove inside and the need to deal with the ice and snow outside. The quietude was broken only by the wonderful music of the insects that was added to by the sounds of the frogs that had come to occupy the fifteen- to twenty-five-foot pond I had built on the property. The sounds of civilization were so far away down off the ridge.

These years of weekend residence in this wonderful house caused us to be focused on the Shenandoah Valley as a potential final place for our lives, and as a result of our inquiries, we did become residents of Westminster-Canterbury in Winchester.

Possession of this house with its two bedrooms, good kitchen, spacious living room with a skylight overhead, and two bathrooms had made it possible for us to entertain family and friends upon numerous occasions there. These warm memories remain with us. Our overnight guests were family members from our daughter's married family and my nephew and his family from Georgia, and my sister and her husband from Oregon. There were also members from our so called extended family of friends who had lived overseas with us under various conditions and whose children were with them on these occasions. Included were friends who were able to stay over with us and enjoy the nearby lake on the ridge, including David Sackson, the violinist from New York and his wife Nancy. They reciprocated by inviting Haya and me to stay with them at their respective homes in upstate New York and Long Island.

Thus, as these two decades approximately were rounded out for Haya and me, the experiences and memories of a lifetime that matched the work and accomplishments of my intelligence career, which was recognized in the Lifetime Achievement Award granted by the Association for Intelligence Officers to me in November 2006. Upon receiving it, I knew perfectly well that it was deserved at least as much by my wife, Haya, and our daughter Ann who had both contributed so much to the patterns and accomplishments of my career.

The Reckoning

There you tower, emperor high
Looking down on your forest vessels
Strong, oh yes, and standing still
Survivor of so many years and sea-
sons

Your roots run deep into the soil
That gives your limbs great strength
Their reach overshadowing all com-
petitors
For your space and the sun's warm
rays

In the spring, your branches glow with
charm
That soon brings out those promising
leaves
Which flourish into the emerald robe
That you yearly wear with such pride

Summer and autumn feed that glory
That you justly show to all
Before there comes that reckoning
With nature's humbling winter call

And looking up, all the forest folk
Bemoan your naked state
And watch in awe as snow and ice
Trim back your overbearing limbs

Fenton Babcock

Ridge of Shadows

Sun shadows, moon shadows
Lengthen and retreat
Shadows of a past regret
Shadows of a smile

Shadows of a long day's night
Of pain and sorry full
Shadows from a breaking dawn
Of hope, and love, and truth

Shadows changing with the sun's
Bright and equalizing rays
Where tall and short come to cast
At noon the same profile

This hallowed ridge of shadows past
Looking down on Blue and Gray
Ranks of fighting men who crossed
The valley's bloodied floor

Long before, the settlers came
And saw atop the ridge
Shadow forms of Indians
Watching with intent

Intent to keep nature's gifts
Safe from white man's spoil
Safe from flora, fawn, and fowl
Safe from ringing axe and hoe

So we this heritage must keep
In heart and mind and soul
And as the evening shadows fall
Turn to the stars and say

A thankful prayer for nature's gifts
Of summer sun, and winter snow
The hope of spring, the glory of fall
On the ridge of shadows cast for all

For all who come with reverence
For nature's gifts to man
The right to stand with arms out-
stretched
To feel, and love, and look with awe

Fenton Babcock

As with Evelyn and her husband, Art Valotto, at that time, our attention was beginning to focus on the thought of a life care community organizations. In my case and Haya's, our attention was focused after much driving around in rural areas upon Winchester as a city with considerable attraction. After viewing a slide show presentation by the marketing representative of Shenandoah Valley Westminster-Canterbury, we then drove directly to the site, which then consisted only of a meadow, but upon seeing the model produced by the developing firm, we made our down payment and got in line for one of the new cottages to be built in 1995. Thus, we were afforded the distinct pleasure of forming our own yard and gardens and contributing to the atmosphere being formed by the residents at this new life care community. We became very comfortably settled in. Haya became directly involved in increasing the amount of volunteer work done by residents. I became involved in some of the developmental projects on the grounds.

One of these was the project to restore seventy feet of a 200-year-old stone wall surrounding the Memorial Grove. The wall was in a state of disrepair. This brought me directly into contact with Art Valotto, the husband of Evelyn, while working shoulder to shoulder on that rather large job in the woods. At the same time, Evelyn and I were brought together in two singing groups and performed a duet on more than one occasion. We met socially over dinner, which included her family from Warrenton, Virginia.

Having already transferred from our cottage into one of the apartments in the main building due to Haya's declining health, Art's direct assistance to us increased considerably. Later, after I lost my sight with a stroke that occurred on the work site in the woods, I was dependent upon his driving me to a nearby facility for blood work. He was also instrumental in moving our belongings from the apartment to the Assisted Living unit when that change was needed. Art and I, both having been involved directly in combat action off Japan in 1945, it was understandable that we would work well together.

The family atmosphere developed at Westminster-Canterbury was strong during this time. The management was working well to maintain this to the best of their ability. In the case of my wife and me, we would simply take her wheelchair and go amongst the cottages, stopping in time to time with the Valottos and other friends with our cat, Shadow, riding on Haya's lap while in her wheelchair.

Throughout this period of change from cottage independent living to independent apartment living to assisted living in a separate building known as Wappacomo Hall, one of the dominant memories is that of the assistance given to us by our daughter Ann. Haya had chronic pulmonary disease and congestive heart failure during which made her breathing a major problem. She required medication at all times and, ultimately, the use of oxygen. She was literally not able to carry on any of the work in moving, and Ann made herself available to assist me in that. Her assistance was absolutely critical in handling our family finances for us. After my eyesight loss, it made it impossible for me to read documents or sign them properly, so she took on the role of "business manager," as she liked to call it.

The assistance of Westminster-Canterbury medical staff was absolutely outstanding and made all the difference along the way. They gave assistance to us in the handling of medications. Toward the end of Haya's life, they helped in the decision making about her movement to hospice care, and, ultimately, to the constant critical assistance section of Westminster-Canterbury. Once in a separate room, Haya began to exhibit the "Sundowner's Syndrome" actions of rejecting my presence and also becoming determined to get out of the unit. The outstanding nursing staff there handled the situation perfectly, including an explanation to me that my assistance was not desirable, and that I should leave the quarters for a while and return only after Haya's condition had calmed down. At the end of Haya's life, Ann was unfortunately not there. She was putting her son in college in Montana. She had asked that her in-laws, Harry and Doris Walters, step in should anything serious occur. They were so very helpful assisting in the last hours of Haya's life. In addition to all the support they offered me, they were able to get hold of Ann by phone. Haya was thus able to hear Ann's voice in the last moments of her life, although she herself could not speak to Ann.

Her lifetime of smoking almost certainly contributed strongly to the downward turn of her health. She had tried to break the habit of smoking more than once but was not successful. Finally, when living in assisted living, the staff convinced her that she must use the patch approach and that did bring an end to the smoking, which could not accompany her use of oxygen.

Over the fifty-five years of our marriage, I did not undertake to strongly discourage her and certainly did not try to force her to break her habit of smoking. I explained that to Ann. I explained that Haya simply carried too heavy a load over the wartime years in Germany and, subsequently, in supporting me through my whole career in intelligence. She had earned the right to continue that outlet for herself of smoking if she truly wanted to.

My experience in the Death and Dying Program in New York had equipped me to address the question of dying with Haya and she welcomed that. In fact, she herself initiated a number of questions about death and dying and wanted my help in addressing them. In the end, when she asked me to release her to end her days of living with me in this way, it led her, in her words, "to release me" to have the most wonderfully satisfying life I could have for myself from that point on. She then reached to the cupboard beside her chair, took down the painting of sunflowers that she so treasured because of her childhood in Germany, and she handed that picture to me in what I knew was a clear indication that she recognized for me, the best prospect would be to perhaps build a new life with Evelyn Valotto. That was because Evelyn had so thoughtfully brought to Haya armfuls of the gloriosa daisies (black-eyed Susans) that Haya had come to equate in her mind with the sunflower she had known so well and loved so much in Germany.

Our assistant rector at Christ Episcopal Church, Ann Kirchmeir, responded so warmly to my request for meditation and a chance to talk about my future. She also clearly identified Evelyn to me as one to whom I might well turn to in the next phase of my life. That was because Evelyn had brought Haya and me to the Pilgrim's Chapel at Christ Church for the services on Wednesdays, to which Haya became so attached.

In the end, I came to feel truly blessed that the loss of my sight, thus ending my career, had enabled me to provide my wife, Haya, the assistance she deserved and needed at the end of her life

Fenton receives Retirement Awards from the CIA

Chapter Seventeen

<u>You Have No Sight</u>

*This chapter opens with a poem that is followed by a
detailed sight-loss experience and closes with a brief
epithet.*

<u>You Have No Sight</u>

*When she passed that judgment on me
I first thought the doctor must be wrong
True, I could not see beyond the end of the hallway
But I did not realize there was a chart
That meant that the letters on the chart
Could not be seen by me at all*

*Thus began my entry into
The world of legal blindness
How surprised I was to find that this world of expected loss
Turned out to be a world of gain*

*True, I don't see the way I did before
But now I see them much better
How much more correct did I find
My mind's eye to be measuring for me
The true character of my wife, for example*

The source of all my happiness
My memory told me that she was beautiful
But now I see her full beauty

She is seen through a glass darkly
And as if I am swimming beneath the surface

Ever reaching for the light
But not really wanting to reach it
To look for the glare is just blinding to me
Full darkness is however not better
So I settle for both and cope as I can
Relying upon truths to get me through

I read people's character now I believe
Better than I ever could before
Dependent now upon the tone of their voices
And not the words they use for me

Fortunately now I can remember the voices
And often speak their names in reply
How gifted I am now to have this better hearing
With a wife who sings each day into being
And carries me through each day of my life
And puts me to sleep with her lullabies

Nature has also taught this blind man
To treasure each day of his life
And make of it something that really counts
For himself, his family and his community

For himself, he is now determined never to fall again
Particularly from poorly directed pride
Now, too, effort to strengthen my body
And clear my mind for moving into the future
Concepts, thoughts and ideas
That might bring a state forever

I'm working to tune my senses in such a way
That they will overcome my loss of sight
Tactile sense has already given me
Increased clarity of appreciating my wife

When touching her beautiful full, soft long hair
I in my mind's eye see her more clearly
Than anybody else could
In the attention that she gives to her appearance
I literally see the value that I place on her

In the time and effort that she gives to her health
I see the value that she shares with me on our life together
And in all of the many ways that she helps me
I see all the way into her heart

In the ways that my blindness caused me to reach
Up to Evelyn with all the love inside me
In my poetry I will try to find those ways
To give her strength and comfort

And in reaching out to the community
We try to find ways to write
Our story in truth and depth
That will have helpful meaning
For those whose circumstances
Might be comparable to ours

In sum, we have formed a new life
To complement our previous ones
Building upon our lives of commitment and work
We have reached our rainbow's end
And have our God given opportunity
To find life's true peace and utmost value
That lies in the sharing of love

With this poetic introduction, I now feel free to share some facts and details about my so called "sightless" life. To begin with, I can, in fact, see a little bit in both of my eyes, but limitation is great indeed, and the amount I can see is clearly enough to get me into trouble.

There were four neuro-ophthalmologists consulted by me over approximately the first year who shared the same conclusion. The damage to my central optical nerve was such that it was irreparable, and it would affect both of the eyes. I knew soon enough that they had been affected differently and that I would thus have to take that into account as I tried to see with my eyes. Both eyes seemed to be affected in the same way by light and darkness. The brightness as such that it was truly blinding and is to be avoided and dealt with special glasses that I wear. The overall impression in my mind is that I am viewing, when I can, through a body of water in which I am swimming. People and things that register on my eyes are almost constantly moving and they will be blanked out as the eyes get tired and focus declines to zero.

With reference to the early months of discomfort, I would have to say that circumstances have improved greatly. In those early months I was faced with hallucinations that were bothersome indeed. For example, the appearance on the floor of our apartment of the oxygen hoses that were swirling around were a real hazard and the worst part was that they weren't there. The tubes had been lying there when Haya was drawing on the oxygen from her main tank, but when they were put away they were still there as far as my eyes were concerned. For me it was a matter of trying to step over them and this was complicated by the appearance of snow-white substance that did not exist but appeared to be covering the whole floor space in our apartment in the Assisted Living Building. At night, the hazard was one of lying in bed and being attacked by moths coming toward me on all sides and being unable to bat them away in any way, shape or form. Again, they did not exist, but in mind they were most certainly there and were a barrier to quiet sleep.

Without question, however, the most threatening hallucination was the one that I relayed in mind back to the origin of the eyesight loss, which was when I was struck down when working on the stone wall restoration project at Westminster-Canterbury. I collapsed right beside the wall. Apparently, the picture of the wall was frozen on my neuro-optical nerve, and so in the subsequent months, when I would try to walk outside, I would suddenly be faced by a wall of stone.

Again, it did not exist, but there it was right in front of me and I was faced with the question of whether or not I should try to walk into it, through it, around it, or just back away and give up. Since that option was clearly not available in my mind, I would always put out my hands to feel my way. When riding in a car, I would have the distinct impression that the car was driving right into a solid wall of stone. Of course, that did not occur and the threat did not exist, but in my mind it was most definitely right there and was a burden when I was moving in the car, and it forced me to make it clear to the driver that this really was dealt with by driving slowly.

Fortunately, within approximately two to three months, these hallucinations faded away and disappeared. Testing by a specialist sent from the central low vision office at the old hospital became clear that my two eyes were very different in their focus. That required simply not using one eye or another or alternating as the circumstances required, and therefore, only seeing through the London fog shroud that always surrounded me. At one point, in response to the encouragement from my new life with my new wife, Evelyn, I undertook trying to play the piano again. I went alone into the room where there was a piano and attempted to sit at the keyboard to play, and found that I was getting so sick to my stomach from the fact that the keyboard had almost a forty degree angle; I simply stopped. The dark humor in that fact is that last piece that I had played at the International House at Yale in my graduate year was "As Time Goes By."

The fall taken by me down fourteen steps in November 2008 demonstrated to me that need for consistent care in my walking and my dependence upon help from other people could not be refused. Now in my constant use of a walker, the danger of falling has been reduced and within the home that I have in this cottage with my wife, I am able to maneuver in and around obstacles that are recognizable in one way or another. That recognition usually comes through contrast of dark items against a white background or the opposite. Eating has been facilitated by the availability of dark plates and other containers. Having them blue in color is a real help. Balance continues to be a problem in terms of the danger of spilling liquid from a cup that is filled too full.

Some two years ago, at an earlier stage in my low vision problem, I was able to benefit from the special equipment that was obtained by the assisted living department, which magnified pictures and text. With that I was able to identify large photographs and read new lines of text before it would fade away. Over the past year, I came to realize that that was no longer possible, and I have not been able to enjoy any text or photographs and must rely completely on my wife to help me identify things by describing them to me.

Strangely enough, however, I have found that in my sleep I see things and people and circumstances and places very clearly. I envision myself traveling in automobiles and I also find myself on the tennis court literally playing tennis effectively. In my sleep, reading text, I found there is a great deal of duplication and the text usually appears in slightly jumbled short sections.

However, regrettably to accept the prediction by the specialist that my eyesight will steadily degrade, I have undertaken to make the very most I possibly can of my present capabilities and circumstances. Composing sentences and chapters for this book, dictating it into a recorder, and then going over the transcribed text with my wife has certainly provided important stimulation, and has constituted a specific outlet for me.

My thoughts along poetic lines seem to have been increasing under these circumstances and an actual production of poetry clearly has a definite benefit for me. A continuation of my singing has been possible as a member of the so called "Sophisticates" group and the procedure is simply that of listening to a song that they want to sing alone or in duet with Evelyn and practicing it repeatedly until it is initially prepared for presentation to the monthly music club.

In this brief epithet, I undertake to present the three lifetime gifts that I hold most dearly.

First is the sound, promising upbringing given to me by my family members identified in Chapters One and Two, which extinction was instantly threatened in combat during the war and then returned by heavenly hand to me.

My second cherished gift is the lifetime of quality education and highly valued challenge provided by government subsidy and assignment as loyally supported and advanced by my late wife, Haya, and our strongly supportive daughter Ann.

My third is the gift of intertwining the intellects that Evelyn and I bring to bear on subject matter that gives the final value we seek in our lives with love and hope for the future.

Truly, a Caring Community
A to Z at Shenandoah Valley Westminster-Canterbury

My recollections of fifteen wonderful years at the Westminster-Canterbury life care community in Winchester, Virginia, go over A to Z in the alphabet. This record begins in early 1985, when my late wife, Haya, and I attended an evening program at our St. John's Episcopal Church in Langley, Virginia, where there was a slide show presentation on SVWC. The lecture by the very attractive lady representing this newly planned life care community ended with an invitation to visit by bus the site in Winchester.

Upon arrival during the following daytime trip, we were favored by a ride in a convertible car driven by Bill Lawrence with his wife, who donated the forty-one acres for the construction. We were driving through a meadow with nothing to see, but we could enjoy the beautiful surroundings. From there we went by bus to the old mall in Winchester and at the First Presbyterian Church and were shown the architect's model of the planned facility. Our subsequent family discussion included Ann, who by that time had already graduated from college and was beginning to start her own life. We covered the various factors, which had pointed us in the direction of considering this new type of life. In my case, the factor most pressing was the recollection of my parents who had chosen to end their lives in a house at a wonderful place near the ocean. They did not consider living in a life care community. They were fortunate enough to have the financial means to provide the round-the-clock nursing they required in the final years of their lives.

Haya and I felt that we were in good enough health condition to qualify for entrance at Westminster-Canterbury, and we knew that we were not in the financial status that would permit us to have our own nursing care at home. The facilities described to us for the life care community were certainly attractive, and we were intent upon finding a place for ourselves that would be no more than one hour away from our daughter. That point proved critical in the subsequent years of our residence at SVWC.

On the matter of financing this change of life, we were fortunate in having to sell our old farmhouse in Vienna, Virginia, and also the Oakton, Virginia, apartment. In the course of those changes, we had placed ourselves on the futures list at SVWC, which had already developed for itself an attractive reputation in the Winchester area. Having overcome a financial set back by starting the construction of individual cottages to compliment the main buildings at SVWC, we determined the optimum time for us to enter that life care community was to be upon the selection of one of the newly established cottages. Since our deposit, in the amount of $2,000, had been on the books at SVWC for close to ten years at this point, we had a high priority position on the futures list. The result was our having first choice of the cottage plan for the new road called Elderberry Drive. We were able to go out and view the place on the ground where it would be built. Haya was able to come daily to observe the process and progress of our new cottage, while I was working during the day. For four months, we were occupying a retreat house that we had built ten years before on the Blue Ridge. It was about twenty minutes away from Westminster-Canterbury, and we had the pleasure of seeing our cottage grow from nothing to a truly attractive place. As the first residents in this cottage, we had the privilege of planning and developing the gardens and surroundings. That brought a lot of satisfaction to me. The staff planted certain trees at our request and we planted the additional ones that we chose and paid for, and the backyard became truly a beautiful place. At the side of the house, I began building a stone wall. The head of the maintenance staff, Ernie Racey, contributed a load of stone brought from his property in nearby West Virginia. He would dump it on the front lawn and I would work on the wall. As the pile diminished, he would bring another load the next day or two. This made a nice garden wall within a matter of a few weeks.

In that same vein, when I had time on weekends to work around the place, I undertook to restore a fifteen-foot-long, very old, tumbled-down wall at the entrance of Elderberry Drive. Later, this method would be used on the seventy-foot-long wall surrounding the Memorial Grove when working on it with my neighbor, Arthur Valotto.

Identified as "Independent Living" residents in one of the cottages, we developed a very delightful life over a period of six years before our move to the main buildings. We found cottage life to be truly delightful, quiet, and enjoyable, and within contact with neighbors in the duplex cottages. We would go to the main buildings for dinner in the main dining room or the cafeteria. There were even invitations to have pre-dinner drinks with residents in their own apartments or in one of the main buildings. The size of Westminster-Canterbury at that time was such that almost everyone felt that they knew their neighbors and the "happy hours" were indeed very enjoyable.

This first phase of life at Westminster-Canterbury was marked by Haya enjoying the quietude of the cottage and the company of our cat, which we called Shadow, who lived to a total of twenty years. Haya and Shadow enjoyed watching out the back bay window of the cottage the activity of all of the birds and animals, which included fox, rabbits, deer, and a ground hog.

Snow, of course, made the backyard particularly beautiful. We had planted five hemlocks that wore those snowy bows so beautifully. The weeping willow supplied by Westminster-Canterbury grew to a very large size while we were still there.

As this six-year phase moved on, I had a radical prostatectomy and Haya began to suffer from COPD (chronic obstructive pulmonary disease) and congestive heart failure. As a result, the time came for a committee of selected members from the staff to recommend that we move to one of the main buildings that would put us in direct contact with the clinic. A public moving van was hired by us to move our belongings. With the incomparable assistance of Ann and members of her family, the move was carried off without great difficulty. We settled into the new life of apartment living in Shenandoah Hall at Westminster-Canterbury. In the subsequent nine years, Haya and I would be residents of Assisted Living and the Health Care. Following the death of Haya, I am married to Evelyn, whose husband, Art, had died a year and a half after Haya. It is only after my marriage to Evelyn that I am now back in the Independent Living cottages that I so loved.

In the course of these five separate phases of life within Westminster-Canterbury, I experienced the whole pattern of life available here, the benefits and the opportunities that are truly unique. As a co-leader of the annual "evening of poetry" that I helped organize and held for ten years, we uncovered a significant amount of talent that otherwise might not have come forward, and we all learned to appreciate poetry in many different forms.

As a member of three different singing groups at Westminster-Canterbury, I was experiencing the joy of singing as a member of duets with my wife and also a member of the larger men's group called Westbury Boys and Evie, featuring Evelyn along with the rest of us. Evelyn and I helped to found and develop a much larger mixed singing group called the Westbury Choristers Chorus.

In addition, for close to two years, we organized and helped to develop the so called Silver Liners singing group within the Blue Ridge Hall section of the Health Center.

It was in the Fitness Center at Westminster-Canterbury that Evelyn and I actually met for the first time and in which we continue, at the time of writing this book, to enjoy the helpful life that we find here. Coming as we do each evening from our cottage to the main building complex for dinner, we enjoy the company of several close friends at a table in Morgan's Tavern, which is part of the new Vitality Center that overlooks directly the very delightful walking garden outside in which there is a continuously flowing stream.

Throughout this whole experience, perhaps the most dominant theme has been the family atmosphere that is generated and perpetuated by the residents and staff. The staff thinks of us as family members and we reciprocate that feeling. Once a year, close to Christmas, the employees receive a gratuity gift check, contributed by the residents inasmuch as tipping throughout the year is not allowed at Westminster-Canterbury.

My direct benefit from the quite unique family atmosphere in relationship between residents and staff began at the time of my loss of sight in the fall of 2004. I was able to focus my attention on assisting Haya in our life in Shenandoah Hall. I had taken on the task of getting Haya and my evening dinner tray at the cafeteria. The cafeteria staff obviously assisted in selecting the food and making sure that I got safely through the cafeteria and headed back down the hall toward our apartment. They all pitched in to make sure that we received our dinners, and that they were placed in such a way that I could carry them safely back to the apartment. My relationship with some of these staff members became very warm and it was to carry on over subsequent years, when I would have contact with them in the Assisted Living section, in the Bistro or Morgan's Tavern.

Another staff who began to directly benefit me and affect my life at Westminster-Canterbury was that in the Therapy section, which was known of at that time as the Wellness Center. The occupational therapist led me in the subsequent weeks and months through the old experience of learning about low vision and how the available facilities and materials could benefit me. She periodically assisted me by resetting my talking wrist watch and, later, also daily redressing the wound in my leg developed from falling down a flight of fourteen steps. This went on for many, many weeks.

My almost one-year-long recovery from the damage received from that fall was provided by the physical therapist in that same center. His wise advice and patience in dealing with me over that long, extended period of recovery meant a great deal to me. That long recovery process began in the Assisted Living section called Wappacomo Hall. I was observed for one week there before being transferred back to the life care section. I felt very much at home in Wappacomo Hall for that recovery because my wife and I had already lived there for two years. The assistance we received from the nursing staff was outstanding. The nursing staff brought warmth and nearly a family atmosphere that made all the difference in the final stage of my life with Haya. So later, when I needed to recover from my broken back, the family-like relationship with that staff made a great deal of difference.

Throughout the course of Haya's last months and also in the period of recovery from my own accident, the relationship with the nursing staff in Dogwood Court and also Laurel Court, and the leading staff of the nursing department was truly outstanding. That was also greatly facilitated by the concern of the chaplain and social worker.

Subsequently, when using the Fitness Center, including the swimming pool, it was the staff there who had made a difference in working with Haya. Well aware of my vision problem and the need for my recovery from that fall down the stairs, staff members and administrators have gone out of their way to assist in the recovery.

Last, but by no means least, I have been consistently conscious of the warmth and effectiveness of the maintenance and grounds staff that have been so responsive for requests for help of various kinds.

Having lived through three successions of chief executive officers leading Westminster-Canterbury, I am convinced in my mind that care and effectiveness of this group has been totally and truly outstanding. We all know, of course, that their success has come through the selection of truly outstanding leaders at the division level. The clearest evidence of that lies in the happiness and contentment of the staff members who perform all of the daily activities here at Westminster-Canterbury. That, in turn, is seen in the preparedness of the residents who come forward and volunteer to undertake and carry out the additional activities here that supplement the work of the staff and those activities that contribute so much to the richness of life here.

Family Tributes

Tribute and Appreciation for Haya Babcock

Haya arrived in the United States as an immigrant from Germany in February 1950. She settled into the Yale University community as a secretary and it was not very long before she began to move upward in the university staff and reach the choice position of the secretary for the master of one of the residential colleges making up Yale University.

It was natural for her to make new friends at the Yale International House. She was comfortable there amongst the twenty-four residents representing thirteen different countries in all the different languages spoken there.

In the course of the many evening conversations with Haya's sponsor for immigration, who was then serving on the faculty at Yale University in the German department. I learned a great deal about her wartime years in Germany. There they brought out the horrors of the almost daily bombing, which directly affected her family, as well as the period in which she was transferred to Austria and the train she was on was strafed by an Allied aircraft. It was in Vienna, Austria, however, where her most critical experience took place, in which she was confined in the basement of her quarters by a unit of occupation forces from the Soviet Union. Violation of her by individual members of the unit ended only after one week by the interference of a priest from a nearby convent.

Upon her return to Germany, she was quickly in the ranks of Germans assisting the Allied Forces, and because of her bilingual capabilities, she was given direct access to very sensitive information in the Berlin Document Center. Within two years, it had become evident that her personal danger should be ended by immigration to the United States.

Within five years after our marriage, in October of 1950, Haya and I were on our way to East Asia for the pursuit of my career that was strongly supported by her.

Upon our arrival for our retirement years in Westminster-Canterbury, Haya assumed a responsibility for coordinating some volunteer efforts. Within five years, however, it became clear that her health was failing steadily and she was told by her doctor that she had early onset dementia. Haya's strong character came out as the time waned for the rest of her life and she literally undertook with me to examine the prospects for her death and how she would deal with that.

Drawing upon my experience in New York City helping terminal cases, Haya and I were able to develop a useful dialogue, and in the course of that, she said that she would release me from any responsibilities that I would have and I should turn my attention to finding the most beneficial and happy life for myself. She made it very clear that I would best turn my face to Evelyn Valotto as a prospect for the companion for the remainder of my life. It was only in the last stage of her illness that there was reflection of her experience during the war in Vienna, Austria. One day, as I sat in her room in the life care section, she drew her walker up in front of her to fend me off anyone who might approach, and she called out to the nurse to have the authorities remove me from her room. As I began to depart, she struck me with her fist beside my head and made it very clear that this was her fighting back against previous threats of some kind.

In the memorial service provided for Haya after her death in August 2007, the trip was made to recapture some of this background of commitment and strength on her part in the face of considerable challenge over many years. In the same effort, there was a recounting of her leadership in developing our small family, and the raising of a fine daughter and the accompaniment of her husband during his difficult period of loss of his eyesight.

Tribute and Appreciation
For Ann Babcock Walters

While Haya and I were in New Haven as I was completing my graduate work, we engaged in testing at the Yale Medical School on the question of the advisability of having a child of our own. Because Huntington's chorea was in Haya's family history, it was decided that it would not be desirable to have a child of our own. That decision was carried with us during our three years in the first assignment overseas in Taiwan.

As the tour there in Taiwan, at Tung Hai University, came to an end, it was agreed that Haya would precede me back to the United States by way of Europe and explore the prospects for adopting a child. Several cable exchanges over the next few weeks while I was still in Taiwan made it clear that progress was being made in Germany.

On my arrival in Germany, it became clear that this German Red Cross adoption was becoming a reality because of two things: as recognition of the exceptional, sensitive contribution made by Haya's father during the war and also as a response to the specific request by Haya, who was a native of Germany.

In June 1958, the beautiful Ann Christiane Babcock became our daughter. As with her mother, Haya, before her, Ann came to the United States and became an American citizen. Shortly thereafter, we were on our way to the exotic orient.

In the four years of her life in Hong Kong she became fluent in Chinese and developed as a beautiful youngster. Upon departure heading back to the United States, we felt that our Ann had benefited from this different cultural experience, and that it would be valuable for her in many ways. We felt very fortunate in providing this opportunity for her.

During much of the period in Hong Kong, for example, Ann had the opportunity to spend every day with the grandchild of the servant who had arrived in the middle of the night as a refugee from mainland China, a youngster the same age as she who spoke no English. Ann became very comfortable with the Shanghai dialect that he spoke and, almost every day, was seen with him at the table in the kitchen practicing writing Chinese.

Our servant family of three people, two parents and a daughter, plus the grandson, was an exceptional family. This exposure for Ann brought her a good understanding for the deference typical of most Chinese and the loyalty that they displayed at all times, along with their practicability.

The four years in Hong Kong also brought Ann in these first four years of her life exposure to our extended family friends from the Foreign Service and Intelligence organizations and our British friends there, and also the many Chinese who we came to know very well. Many of the American children of our friends were growing up together in this foreign-broadening perspective that they were to benefit from later in their lives.

Later, when we were living near Washington, DC, we were lucky to have a visit to us by Haya's father, Friedrich Vorwerk. I accompanied Haya's father to Philadelphia for him to receive an award from the German government presented by the former head of the Allied Occupation Forces. It revealed to me the special attention that had been given during the acquisition of Ann's adoption.

It was not long before we were headed back to Taiwan again for a three-year tour in the capital of Taiwan. There, fortunately, Ann was able to have a good beginning education in the American school.

Upon our return to Virginia, we were fortunate to have my nephew, Brian Babcock, come to live with us. He became, in effect, almost a brother to Ann. Brian had a very favorable influence on Ann during the nearly one year that he lived with us. It helped her develop a sense of family.

Ann's middle school and secondary education went well and prepared her for attending college, which also went well, with her gaining a variety of experiences and responsibilities. In the following years, Ann married Harry Walters and they raised two fine, strong young men, and as Ann thought, she has found the warmth of an expanding family. The members of that family have assisted Haya and me by pitching in on numerous occasions, which were greatly appreciated.

The developing closeness of Ann's friendship with my wife, Evelyn, has been highly encouraging to me, and at the same time, Ann has found, through her contact with Evelyn's family, another brother. Merle Fallon is an accomplished attorney in Northern Virginia and he and his wife are raising a fine family of two very attractive and promising young ladies.

In retrospect, I remember particularly November 4, 2006, when I received the Lifetime Achievement Award from the Association for Intelligence Officers. I remember it particularly because Haya has passed away at that point and Ann accompanied me on that occasion and sat next to me at the head table. As the time came for me to step forward and receive the award before the group of some 300 Intelligence Officers, it was clear in my mind that it was truly Haya and Ann who deserved a large share of that award. It was during my career years that they had to adjust to my full commitment to the work with the Central Intelligence Agency. Both had supported me the best they could. Ann, however, had stepped forward many times to directly assist me and Haya. And meanwhile, she was proceeding in a very commendable steady way to advance her career and her family life in a pattern of very definite accountability. She clearly learned the lessons taught to her back in Hong Kong regarding taking care of one's family and being practical.

Evelyn and Fenton enjoy dancing

A New Persona

As my Aunt Corinne Babcock had opened for me the whole world of graduate studies, I found from my Grandmother Briggs an opening on the world of Chinese history and literature. Taking the trolley from Pasadena, California, to Los Angeles to visit my Grandmother Briggs, I therefore had only fairly short periods of exposure to her and any influence but it came to me at a critical time, just before I entered the service. During my three years of naval service in the Pacific, my focus on China was sporadic, but in retrospect, it was focused sharply on the question of the Chinese as a people undergoing great stress and responding in a special way to that.

As a result, therefore, upon graduation in 1950 as an undergraduate at Yale, as I began studying the Chinese language, my focus became that upon the Chinese that I knew and worked with as individuals. The philosophical construct of "Ai Chin," translated as "enduring love," was made clear to me by my professor at Yale University in the language school and after service as a construct to be clarified in my relationships with various Chinese over the subsequent years. It was natural then for me, upon the loss of Haya after fifty-five years of marriage, to turn to that concept of Ai Chin in thinking about my own future.

With the guidance of the assistant rector at Christ Episcopal Church in Winchester, namely the Reverend Anne Kirchmeir, it was important for me to examine my own base in terms of my own culture and family upbringing and then ask whether it was firm enough for me to stand on it and begin to think toward the future. After concluding that I had very fortunately a firm foundation in my life, I was able to responsively and intellectually look around me in the circle of friends amongst the residents at Westminster-Canterbury to see if there were some bases for communication that would be important for me in thinking about my own future. My friendship with Evelyn Valotto had been growing fairly steadily over the last previous two years when we were singing together in two different singing groups and I was seeing her as a spouse of Arthur Valotto who was working with me shoulder to shoulder on the restoration of the old wall surrounding the Memorial Grove.

Upon the death of Art Valotto, Evelyn thus entered the same situation that I was in, in terms of addressing the future and the question of whether communication between the two of us was an exchange that would strengthen our relationship in a positive way or not.

It was not long before we recognized that we both had firm bases on which to stand in terms of our upbringing and also through the formation of our careers that had extended over many years and we were, therefore, confident that communication between the two of us was likely to be promising, and as we continued in doing exactly that, we found that there was, indeed, a great deal to exchange between us.

My participation in the memorial service that was held before the assembled residents had been well received. I spoke about Art Valotto as a close colleague, not just in the volunteer work at Westminster-Canterbury but also in reference to the wartime experience in which we had both participated, in the action off the Japanese homeland. To test our own reaction to the idea of a close relationship going well beyond friendship, within the construct of Ai Chin, it was logical for me to visit Evelyn at her cottage as a neighbor and for me to be seen there by neighbors and by members of the staff, and the reaction of my family and Evelyn's family was one of acceptance, too.

On June 16, 2007, in the Pilgrim's Chapel at Christ Episcopal Church, we were married in a simple but beautiful service led by the former rector, Michael Mohn. From that time on, our miracle relationship has strengthened steadily. It was well tested during a period of more than six months, during which, I, Fenton, was recovering from a broken back that had occurred during my fall down a fourteen steps.

During that period, the preparation of this book continued as a useful test of our relationship and it has proven to be a team approach that surely is the key to success in most marriages. Full, frank conversation has also been a very important factor in the success of this marriage. Needless to say, the fact of Fenton's loss of his eyesight and the dependence he has upon Evelyn has been also a good test of the strong relationship we have.

The phrase Ai Chin can be translated in the simplest form as follows: well beyond friendship. It should be further expanded as follows: the phrase should convey a commitment for enduring impact and it should be noted that the concept points toward an actual exchange of love. In our case, Evelyn and I believe that we have found a loving relationship and we are participating in that fully. We believe that we have found ourselves standing in and moving in a love meadow, if you will, and in this situation, we have taken the path toward the horizon that we see ahead of us hand in hand. With both of us having demonstrated pioneer instincts throughout our careers, we find that our inclination is to go well beyond the horizon that lies ahead of us. We believe that in this marriage, we found a matching of our respective intellects. We, therefore, reinforce one another as we entertain and examine questions and subject matter.

The previous chapters include identification of our roots and spelled out the family bases upon which we stood as we moved forward in the realm of professional development and family rearing. Certain parallels began to emerge in developing these accounts of our lives, and as we became neighbors within our life care community. In both of our cases, the deaths of our spouses came after fifty years of marriage, and occurred at approximately the same time. Standing on the firm bases that we were fortunate enough to have in our lives, we were free to look around and begin to think about our future in terms of new relationships. For us, the decision to marry began for us a truly amazing transformation. Change has come, in fact, at a rate and to an extent that we now considered ourselves a transformation to a new persona. A new name has thus emerged for us, which is "Flu-Nonie," which is a contraction of a portion of Evelyn's middle name of Fluella and a version of the middle name that the United States Navy placed upon Fenton since he did not have a middle name upon signing in.

We have chosen the bicycle built for two, the tandem-bike symbol, because of its usefulness in emphasizing the three words of direction, strength, and cooperation. It is in these three dimensions that our lives have become transformed in the last four years. In the case of direction, it was a reach of direction that caused the beginning of a long test of our relationship that has turned out to have been very valuable for us. In this case, I, Nonie, mistakenly took a wrong entrance into a stairwell, fell, and tore up the muscles in my back rather badly. For more than a year, he was thus unable to occupy our marriage bed, and in retrospect, we, Flu and Nonie, agreed that the result was good in the sense that we learned the cost of not having the ability to be closely together on a continuous basis. That brings us to the focus on the word "clutch," which is the relationship that we now engage in every night and find ourselves engaging in when we wake up in the morning, and this is a closeness that has come to have great meaning for us, particularly in light of the uncertainty that anyone at our ages has that the future is unending.

In approximately the same period of more than one year, testing our relationship as a new persona, we found that change in Nonie's vision was to become a definite factor in our relationship. In this case, his vision has gone rather steadily downward as predicted by the ophthalmologist, and obviously, this has called for a steady degree of strength in one sense on his part, and certainly a high amount of support from Flu. In the course of this test, cooperation clearly has emerged as a major factor, and in this case, we have the feeling that we are definitely on the road for success in forming our relationship into a firm one.

It became clear that the idea of publishing our first book about Nonie's career in the Central Intelligence Agency would require very close cooperation. In fact, a teamwork relationship between the two of us. This first book included the very informal, totally unclassified personal estimate that Fenton made about the future development of a triangular relationship within the southern part of China, of Hong Kong, Kuang Tung, and Taiwan section, and the estimate that that will come about gradually and without wartime conflict, of course, remains to be seen. Whether or not that will evolve in the coming years is one that Evelyn and Fenton will be watching closely because the United States does have a treaty with Taiwan that calls for military defense of Taiwan against any communist Chinese aggression. The accomplishment of that co-federal formation in the southern part of China would obviously be an extreme example of Ai Chin in operations, well beyond friendship amongst people's long historical background but people who are directly involved in up-to-the minute relationships with other countries, particularly the United States. The following of such subject matter in an active intellectual way to us is a good example of the new lives that can be sought from old, based upon the experience in the old lives. This is a type of stimulation and satisfaction that we regard to be essential in the new lives, and therefore, a logically and necessarily, almost a required goal, for such new lives. Our instincts that told us originally that our intellect would be potentially inter-relational were probably an important factor in moving toward one another. The team accomplishment of the first book entitled The Mercurial Intelligence Career for Fenton and now on our two lives seeking new lives from old is another example of inter-relationship of the two intellects, which is most satisfying for both of us and obviously essential to the product. It is that very relationship that has been drawn on throughout the production of this second book. We have been fortunate to have our transcription assistants, who are professional people, with the task of recording, listening, and making changes; all add up to quite a commitment of time and effort.

This system has worked well, however, and, in fact, has brought about a tentative decision to plan a third publication built around the doctoral dissertation that Nonie had and a study of the China-US relationship at a time that makes it not only essentially important, but a time in which very interesting information can be drawn upon by us in a way that is now a clear example of our intertwining intellects, and the fact that our horizon and interests are broad indeed, and the interest has depth. For us, teamwork has meant a great deal of communication and a type of communication that has turned out to be truly invigorating for us, because we feel that we were somewhat lacking that in our previous marriages, and for us, the result has been a great deal of free, open conversation on a great variety of subjects and a clear indication, in our minds at least, that the coming years will bring us continued stimulation in terms of the need for intellectual application.

The term of strength has emerged in our relationship as a key attribute, one that we both feel we have, and it is in strength in terms of attraction toward one another. In fact, in our case, we have found that literally every night, when we go to bed, there is a physical clutch embrace that has become a necessity for us, and one that brings us an exchange of strength that we both welcome. It is not accidental that Nonie gave Flu early in our relationship a Chinese name, Wei-Lin, which means grace and strength. Certainly, these attributes are a factor in our relationship that is important.

This chapter is ended with the additions of four original poems written by Nonie, and each of these is designed to further demonstrate the specialization of our relationship as we see it. It is a relationship that is quite unique, and it begins with the first poem, which is titled "They Always Called Me Effie," and is a touching poem about the early days of Flu living and working closely with her brother who was lost during the war. He was killed on the island of Guam as a member of the Marine Corp. Death forms chapters we believe the relationship that existed between these two youngsters at that time, and it also captures the feeling of depth and closeness that was experienced by the family of that son, Merle.

The second poem is entitled "A Soul Restored," which captures the experience of redoing completing the long seventy foot stone wall around the Memorial Grove at Westminster-Canterbury, and the hard work that was required for that with Flu's former husband, Art, directly shoulder to shoulder with Nonie as they worked for many months to find the heavy stones that had been long lost under the dirt floor, and to replace them again to form the one large wall. For Nonie, this wall has special meaning, not just because it was on that work site that he lost his eyesight through the stroke of the central optical nerve, and the fact that working that closely with Art Valotto brought the two together in a kinship that dated all the way back to the combat in the Pacific along the Japanese homeland.

The third poem is entitled "Earth Angel of Mine" and focuses completely on Flu and the very special relationship that Nonie has with her, dating back to the initial contact between the two of them during a long period of time when they were singing together in various groups, and during the time on one occasion at the emergency room at the hospital, the two of them spent the whole day reaching in a very open way that came to characterize their conversation from that point on. That poem is to bring out also the very special attributes that Flu has that make her the angel that has brought new life to Nonie.

The fourth poem is quite different. It is entitled "The Statue Speaks" and describes a particular statue at the Corcoran Gallery in Washington, D.C. that is, indeed, a challenging one for all of those who view it, a very different perspective, and it is one that possibly will come to be a citation in yet another study to be made by Flu-Nonie as they get into the question of China and US relationships. It may be that focus on this subject of concubinage can be a relevant subject in the examining of the acculturation of China that is very important with Americans. It is included here to demonstrate the importance of the open conversational relationship that Nonie and Flu have. Our relationship is distinctly a variation of the type of relationship that we individually knew within our previous marriages. Therefore, it is a change that has to be carefully preserved and carefully handled.

In our minds, therefore, the new lives evolving from old must be demanding to some degree as well as simply satisfying, and, in fact, most of the satisfaction comes from such a demanding situation. One looking, therefore, from the old lives for new lives cannot be looking simply for quietude, but must be looking for stimulation and the responsiveness to a requirement in order to provide the satisfaction that is needed for a successful new life, a new persona.

__Poetry__

They Always Called Me Effie

As always I waited for them to come
And as always at the same time they emerged
Running and skipping down from the school
Toward their home in the valley below

The golden haired little boy always comes running in
my direction
With his sister trailing a little behind,
But not much and twirling a stick
The boy always had something under his shirt
And they both always called out the name
They had given me, Effie

I knew they would always find me in the herd
Because of my funny ear
The one that had been torn a bit
On that wire fence on that funny marker fixed, there
in my ear

It never really hurt me much
But the rest of the herd always looked at me strangely
These two friends of mine never hurt me with their
petting

And they always seemed willing to stand there quietly
And watch as I would eat a sandwich
Brought to me by the little boy

I never understood what they were saying
But they repeated that name which I had come to like
The pretty little girl with the brown hair
Always seemed to be singing

And while the rest of the herd stood back
The three of us enjoyed this quiet time together each
day
Over time and change in the season
I seemed to note the change in these children
They got bigger and a little quieter than when
They had run so friskily down the trail

But they always seemed to be very close
And often held hands together
One year I noticed their books seemed to be bigger
And they talked between themselves more quietly

The boy's voice seemed to be deeper and
His hands on my side seemed stronger
One time much later the girl came alone
And waved for me from a car
When she stopped and talked very quietly
I saw something new in her eyes
It looked to me like a rain drop or two
Had been caught on her face
And the next day I heard that sound
I had heard before coming from across the hill

Not when it could hurt us at all
There were those three loud sounds
That were fired with music
Later that day the now young lady
Came by again

And held out for me to see something flat

I soon recognized that I could see the
Young man now dressed in red and blue
And now the sister was crying
And she held me tight around the neck

A long time before she then went slowly away
When I turned around this time
The herd was closing in as he welcomed me
Much more than before
They don't call me, of course

But if I stand quietly by the road sometimes
I can still hear those youngsters calling to me
Both saying together my name, Effie.

Fenton Babcock

A Soul Restored

There you were all tumbledown
Without form, or height, or length
No way to tell your age or strength
Your role in marking out the past

Then, stone by stone, we brought you back
Into our lives to tell and teach
Your lessons of endurance,
Renewal, and reward

We count your many years of life
With every stone retrieved and laid
By reverent hands to form again
Your character and direction
Somehow, each and every one
Whatever its shape and size
Finds its certain place and adds
Its texture, weight and hue

To reconstruct that good neighbor line
That strong bulwark for Blues and Grays
Where valor, work, and sacrifice
Preserved this hallowed ground

So now we see your soul restored
And receive your gifts outright
Of history's telling lessons
With heartfelt words of thanks

Fenton Babcock

Earth Angel of Mine

So it's true, there really are Earth Angels
Who enter the lives of special people
Those who are prepared to receive and return
The love these special angels bring
It's also true that they often first appear
And then take on the lives to which we are accustomed
So that lives go on in normal ways
And it is only gradually that we come to learn
That we have been especially chosen
To have this little peak into heaven

My special angel first appeared
In the rear window of my car
As it was warmed up to go to work
As she strode so determinedly in her morning walk
Little did I know that she would later be
Determined to contact me
But it was not long before
I decided to make contact with her
So natural forces were at work
To bring us into line for a life together

Married now and living in this lovely little cottage
We are experiencing something of Heaven on earth
Characterized by music, love and history
The music clearly is angelic coming from Evelyn
Including your incomparable opening of the day
And your special Nacht Musik
When we sing together our cat April may not like it
But truly I feel inspired by you, Evelyn

Our love is the kind we have identified
In the philosophy of Ai Chin that which is strongly based
And enables entwining of two people in a way
That then results in the formation of a new persona

Clearly, we both have been gaining warmth that we were
missing
We have been gaining the stimulation that is welcomed by
both of us
And the commitment that is shown in the compromising
And understanding that we were experiencing together
The teamwork on the production of our first book was
Clearly evidence of all that.

Fenton Babcock

The Statue Speaks

*My eye placement in a prominent part of the Corcoran Gallery
caused quite a stir Naturally my reactions to the reaction of those
entering and viewing me were quite extensive*
*Amongst the usual tourists there were the expected expressions
of all kinds.*
*Upon seeing the chains around my ankles and those pulling and
holding my wrists behind my back range all the way from shock
and intrigue to their apparent disgust*

*Among those coming to view this statue entitled "The Captive"
Were some who tarried at length and amongst those groups were
repeaters
From time to time over days or even weeks and amongst those
one particular caught my eye.*

*This man seemingly a government functionary looked me right
in the eye
With evident care and concern at the same time
However I detected an understanding that was exceptional*

*He noted for example that I was content with my status
He detected that I was in my status gaining something unusual
I was gaining freedom from the pressures and concerns of others
He detected that I was not being faced with any prospect of dis-
cipline
That would otherwise counteract a mutual bondage into which
I had entered*

*He very evidently had understanding from history of the rela-
tionship into which I had entered
And He understood the mutual commitment that was part of the
arrangement lying behind my status
And he therefore saw in me the benefits of my status he saw the
truth in my eyes
He saw the calmness in my demeanor and he saw the happiness
in my face*

When I understood that he understood

I came to think of this frequent visitor as a friend
Particularly after I heard him saying something in Chinese he
said "Ai chin"
He having described me as beautiful in the Chinese language
I was struck by his comment to someone else in the crowd
That I was in origin a Ero-Asian

I knew from history that in an emperor's realm
There had been some special interest in Ero-Asian background
Amongst the concubines their somewhat different look from the
average Chinese
Turned out to be in the eyes of some emperors a benefit
Those concubines were thus given special treatment
And that treatment was signified by the mutual bondage into
which they were placed
As a result therefore, the concubines came to have an approach
And an understanding and acceptance of bondage that was truly
outstanding

This then is the message that I have been placed in this gallery
to convey
To those spectators willing to approach me with an open mind
My story thus is one of mutual benefit from mutual acceptance
And mutual commitment in a lasting form

The chains thus signify that relationship
As if I am therefore proud to be standing publicly thus bared
History records that I was adopted into an emperor's family
Of concubines at a very, very young age
As a child I thus wore those very small slippers designed to
Prepare me physically and mentally for bondage
And I thus became accustomed to the pressure and
Ultimately turned to ways to relieve that pressure

And as a young lady I found my freedom from that pressure
Through the relationship which you now see before you in statue
form

Fenton Babcock

Fenton and Evelyn at home at SVWC